Learning Sinatra

Design and deploy your own web application in minutes using Sinatra

Sudeep Agarwal

Manoj Sehrawat

BIRMINGHAM - MUMBAI

Learning Sinatra

First published: April 2016

Production reference: 1220416

Published by Packt Publishing Ltd.
Livery Place
35 Livery Street
Birmingham B3 2PB, UK.

ISBN 978-1-84951-930-4

www.packtpub.com

Credits

Authors
Sudeep Agarwal

Manoj Sehrawat

Reviewer
Ken Taylor

Commissioning Editor
Jonathan Titmus

Acquisition Editor
Nadeem Bagban

Content Development Editor
Onkar Wani

Technical Editor
Danish Shaikh

Copy Editor
Tasneem Fatehi

Project Coordinator
Bijal Patel

Proofreader
Safis Editing

Indexer
Mariammal Chettiyar

Production Coordinator
Arvindkumar Gupta

Cover Work
Arvindkumar Gupta

About the Authors

Sudeep Agarwal is a site reliability engineer at Inmobi with a total of four years of experience in the industry. He was with Directi for 3 years right after finishing his education from NIT Trichy. At Directi, he was a part of the team that wrote one of the most widely used in-house web-based applications; this is where his interest in Sinatra started and he used it to write some of his personal projects. Although he is not writing a lot of web applications at Inmobi, he is still contributing to one of the ORMs—Ruby Object Mapper.

This book would not have been possible without the constant support of my family, friends, and peers. I thank everyone for keeping me motivated and helping me with their suggestions. This book is dedicated to each one of them.

Manoj Sehrawat is an enthusiastic software developer who loves coding and learning new things. He has around 5 years of experience in software development. Manoj holds an MCA from KIIT, Gurgaon and a BCA from IGNOU. Currently, he is the associate technical lead at TravelTriangle. TravelTriangle is India's first full stack holiday marketplace that connects travelers with verified travel agents. Before joining TravelTriangle, Manoj was working with StudyPad and Fizzy Software Pvt Ltd as a senior software developer. His primary focus is the design and construction of scalable and optimized web applications and APIs using a Ruby-based development stack with frameworks such as Ruby on Rails, Sinatra, and others. He is passionate about refactoring, optimizing code, and building scalable solutions with simplicity.

I would like to thank several people who helped and supported me in making this book a reality. First, I want to thank my family and fiancé for having the patience with me for taking yet another challenge, which decreases the amount of time I can spend with them.

I must mention that the PECT team is responsible for having me on the team and giving me the opportunity to write this book. I want to thank three of our editors and technical reviewers who worked on this book.

Finally, thanks to the Sinatra and Ruby community!

About the Reviewer

Ken Taylor has worked in software development and technology for over 15 years. During the course of his career, he has worked as a systems analyst on multiple software projects in several industries as well as U.S. government agencies. He has successfully used Ruby (and DSLs like Sinatra) on multiple projects. Ken previously reviewed the books *RabbitMQ Cookbook* and *RabbitMQ Essentials* by *Packt Publishing*. He is an organizer for Google Developer Groups (GDG) and a member and speaker for both 757 Ruby users and the Hampton Roads .NET (HRNUG) users groups. Ken holds an A.S. in computer science from Paul D. Camp Community College and was awarded a U.S. patent for a real estate financial software product. He is currently working as an independent consultant for Onixle LLC. He lives in Virginia Beach, Virginia with his lovely wife, Lucia, and his two sons, Kaide and Wyatt.

> I would like to thank my family for being a constant support in all of my endeavors.

www.PacktPub.com

eBooks, discount offers, and more

Did you know that Packt offers eBook versions of every book published, with PDF and ePub files available? You can upgrade to the eBook version at www.PacktPub.com and as a print book customer, you are entitled to a discount on the eBook copy. Get in touch with us at customercare@packtpub.com for more details.

At www.PacktPub.com, you can also read a collection of free technical articles, sign up for a range of free newsletters and receive exclusive discounts and offers on Packt books and eBooks.

https://www2.packtpub.com/books/subscription/packtlib

Do you need instant solutions to your IT questions? PacktLib is Packt's online digital book library. Here, you can search, access, and read Packt's entire library of books.

Why subscribe?

- Fully searchable across every book published by Packt
- Copy and paste, print, and bookmark content
- On demand and accessible via a web browser

Table of Contents

Preface

This book will help you understand the basic concepts of Sinatra and build lightweight web applications. The book follows a step-by-step course, right from setting up Ruby and installing Sinatra to inculcating best practices for writing beautiful code. By the end, you will have a running Sinatra app ready and the confidence to write more apps by yourself.

What this book covers

Chapter 1, Introduction to Sinatra, helps you set up Sinatra and see a sample Hello World app, followed by a quick comparison with Rails.

Chapter 2, Introduction to Ruby, is intended for Ruby newbies, which helps in setting up Ruby using rvm and understanding how to write code in Ruby.

Chapter 3, Hello World, helps you write the skeleton of a ToDo app and understand it line by line.

Chapter 4, Modeling the Backend, introduces the concept of ORMs to the user, which is required in order to write the ToDo app.

Chapter 5, Handling HTTP Requests, introduces the concept of controllers and explains how the request-response transaction is implemented.

Chapter 6, Designing the Frontend Layout, introduces HAML and Twitter Bootstrap, which is used to make beautiful user interfaces easily.

Chapter 7, Handling User Data, shows you how to create a form and its necessary attributes, and explains how it works. We will see the importance and usage of the `method` and `action` attributes of a form. We will create a `for` loop to add a List and Items of a list to a single form, where we will see how we can add an array of values to the HTML input. You will also learn how to add items to the form through JavaScript dynamically using a simple dummy template. We will see how to handle data at the backend sent by a user through filling in a form, and discuss validations and the types of validation.

Chapter 8, Connecting to a Database, covers how to connect to a database (MySQL) with various necessary parameters. You will learn how to use the mysql gem with `sequel`. We will also cover how to open and use an interactive console with Sinatra and Sequel and the details of Sequel models with various useful class-level and instance-level methods. We will discuss hooks and callbacks available and associations with eager loading and joins in order to scale and optimize the application.

Chapter 9, Authentication and Authorization, shows you the basics of a session in general and how we can configure it with Sinatra, both with simple and advanced options. We will see the various useful methods of a session object and the meaning of authentication and authorization individually.

Chapter 10, Deploying the App, discusses what deployment is, Heroku, and how we can use Heroku to deploy our app. You will also learn the initial setup steps that we need to do on Heroku, and about various Heroku commands and their billing models.

What you need for this book

A basic knowledge of tools and technologies used to write web applications such as HTML, databases, and others. Previous knowledge of any other dynamic language such as Python might help you, but the book covers an introduction to Ruby for first-timers.

Who this book is for

This book will be useful to someone who wants to write lightweight web applications of any size on their own. Someone who wants to move to Ruby-based frameworks from other languages would also find this book interesting.

Conventions

In this book, you will find a number of text styles that distinguish between different kinds of information. Here are some examples of these styles and an explanation of their meaning.

Code words in text, database table names, folder names, filenames, file extensions, pathnames, dummy URLs, user input, and Twitter handles are shown as follows: "We can include other contexts through the use of the `include` directive."

A block of code is set as follows:

```
[default]
exten => s,1,Dial(Zap/1|30)
exten => s,2,Voicemail(u100)
exten => s,102,Voicemail(b100)
exten => i,1,Voicemail(s0)
```

When we wish to draw your attention to a particular part of a code block, the relevant lines or items are set in bold:

```
[default]
exten => s,1,Dial(Zap/1|30)
exten => s,2,Voicemail(u100)
exten => s,102,Voicemail(b100)
exten => i,1,Voicemail(s0)
```

Any command-line input or output is written as follows:

```
# cp /usr/src/asterisk-addons/configs/cdr_mysql.conf.sample
    /etc/asterisk/cdr_mysql.conf
```

New terms and **important words** are shown in bold. Words that you see on the screen, for example, in menus or dialog boxes, appear in the text like this: "Clicking the **Next** button moves you to the next screen."

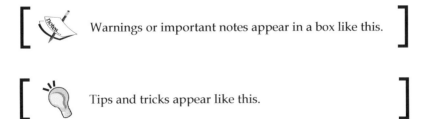

> Warnings or important notes appear in a box like this.

> Tips and tricks appear like this.

Reader feedback

Feedback from our readers is always welcome. Let us know what you think about this book—what you liked or disliked. Reader feedback is important for us as it helps us develop titles that you will really get the most out of.

To send us general feedback, simply e-mail feedback@packtpub.com, and mention the book's title in the subject of your message.

If there is a topic that you have expertise in and you are interested in either writing or contributing to a book, see our author guide at www.packtpub.com/authors.

Customer support

Now that you are the proud owner of a Packt book, we have a number of things to help you to get the most from your purchase.

Downloading the example code

You can download the example code files for this book from your account at http://www.packtpub.com. If you purchased this book elsewhere, you can visit http://www.packtpub.com/support and register to have the files e-mailed directly to you.

You can download the code files by following these steps:

1. Log in or register to our website using your e-mail address and password.
2. Hover the mouse pointer on the **SUPPORT** tab at the top.
3. Click on **Code Downloads & Errata**.
4. Enter the name of the book in the **Search** box.
5. Select the book for which you're looking to download the code files.
6. Choose from the drop-down menu where you purchased this book from.
7. Click on **Code Download**.

Once the file is downloaded, please make sure that you unzip or extract the folder using the latest version of:

* WinRAR / 7-Zip for Windows
* Zipeg / iZip / UnRarX for Mac
* 7-Zip / PeaZip for Linux

Errata

Although we have taken every care to ensure the accuracy of our content, mistakes do happen. If you find a mistake in one of our books—maybe a mistake in the text or the code—we would be grateful if you could report this to us. By doing so, you can save other readers from frustration and help us improve subsequent versions of this book. If you find any errata, please report them by visiting http://www.packtpub.com/submit-errata, selecting your book, clicking on the **Errata Submission Form** link, and entering the details of your errata. Once your errata are verified, your submission will be accepted and the errata will be uploaded to our website or added to any list of existing errata under the Errata section of that title.

To view the previously submitted errata, go to https://www.packtpub.com/books/content/support and enter the name of the book in the search field. The required information will appear under the **Errata** section.

Piracy

Piracy of copyrighted material on the Internet is an ongoing problem across all media. At Packt, we take the protection of our copyright and licenses very seriously. If you come across any illegal copies of our works in any form on the Internet, please provide us with the location address or website name immediately so that we can pursue a remedy.

Please contact us at copyright@packtpub.com with a link to the suspected pirated material.

We appreciate your help in protecting our authors and our ability to bring you valuable content.

Questions

If you have a problem with any aspect of this book, you can contact us at questions@packtpub.com, and we will do our best to address the problem.

1
Introduction to Sinatra

Sinatra is a Ruby-based application framework used to create web applications quickly. It can be used to write simple single-page applications or large and complex ones. Sinatra is very lightweight as it does not include a variety of gems, though the user can include gems as required.

Sinatra is widely used across the globe and has gained a lot of popularity because of its flexibility. It does not follow the **Model-View-Controller** (**MVC**) architectural pattern completely but it is fairly simple to build one on top of Sinatra. Sinatra is a View-Controller framework.

If you have been working with Ruby, you can go ahead and try out the codes; otherwise, you can go ahead with this chapter as we will be covering some basic Ruby in the next chapter. In this chapter, we will be discussing the following topics:

- Model-View-Controller
- How Sinatra is an MVC framework
- When to use Sinatra and when not to use it
- Other popular MVC frameworks

What is MVC?

The **MVC (Model-View-Controller)** is an architectural pattern that divides the application in three parts, namely, the model (the data), view (the user interfaces), and controller (the interconnections between the model and view).

MVC separates the code based on their responsibilities and makes it easier to understand and maintain:

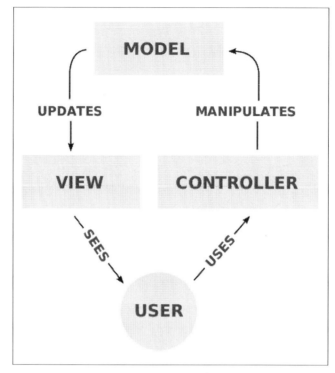

Figure 1-1: MVC components

The concept of MVC will be clearer once we get into the examples using Sinatra.

Installing Sinatra

Sinatra is just another gem and there is no special way to install it. We use the gem install command:

```
$ gem install sinatra
```

This will install the latest version of the Sinatra gem and all its dependencies on your system. To see which version is installed, use the following:

```
$ gem list sinatra
```

Writing your first Sinatra application

Let's see how to write a bare minimum Sinatra application. We will open a new file and write the following code:

```
1 require 'sinatra'
2 get '/' do
3   return 'Hello World!'
4 end
```

Save the file with a .rb extension (say, helloworld.rb) and execute this on the command line:

$ ruby helloworld.rb

This will interpret the code and start the built-in server.

Now, we open the browser and point it to http://localhost:4567.

What did the code do?

```
1.require 'sinatra'
```

This tells the Ruby interpreter to load the Sinatra gem:

```
3 get '/' do
4   return 'Hello World!'
5 end
```

This forms a ruby code-block. Let's understand each line.

```
3. get '/' do
```

This block is invoked when the server receives a get request on the '/' path.

```
4. return 'Hello World!'
```

This will return the 'Hello World!' string to the client.

```
5. end
```

This ends the code-block.

Where is the MVC in this code?

Sinatra does not follow the MVC architecture completely; it is a VC framework. It was mentioned earlier that the model is the data part of the application, view is the user interface, and controller is the interconnection. Now, let's find these parts in the preceding code:

```
1 require 'sinatra'
2
3 get '/' do
4   return 'Hello World!'
5 end
```

Here, line 1 requires just the gem. Lines 3 to 5 define a code-block that is invoked on receiving a `get` request and returns a value. So here, this code-block forms the controller. It controls what to return when a request is received.

The view is the page rendered by the browser. We do not have a separate view here but line 4 defines the contents of the view.

How to achieve MVC using Sinatra

To achieve MVC using Sinatra, we need to pick a database framework and use it with Sinatra. There are many database frameworks available, such as Active Record, DataMapper, Sequel, and others. In the later chapters, we will be working with Sequel.

Sinatra application layout

As Sinatra can be used for applications that can be bare minimum or large and complex, the application structure can grow bigger with the need.

For now, let's stick to the basic layout.

A basic Sinatra application will have a ruby file that has all the controllers defined (for example, `helloworld.rb`).

If we want to have different HTML files (or different views), we should place all such files in the `views` folder.

The layout is as follows:

```
helloworld.rb
views/
```

Naming convention: The main application file is generally named `app.rb` or `website.rb`.

Let's now see how to write views. Views can be written in HTML. However, there are some gems in Ruby that make our lives easier. One of them is HAML.

HAML

HTML Abstraction Markup Language (**HAML**) is a templating engine that helps in writing cleaner and simpler HTML. For example, refer to the following table:

HTML	HAML
<pre><body>
  <div id='comment'>
    <form>
      <input type='text'>
    </form>
  </div>
</body></pre>	<pre>%body
  %div#comment
    %form
      %input{:type => 'text'}</pre>

We can see here how HAML is simpler and neater than HTML.

Installing HAML

The following is the command to install HAML:

```
$ gem install haml
```

Using HAML in a Sinatra application

We will have two files in this case, `helloworld.rb` and `index.haml`.

The layout is as follows:

```
helloworld.rb
views/
        index.haml
```

helloworld.rb
```
1 require 'sinatra'
```

```
2 require 'haml'
3
4 get '/' do
5   haml :index
6 end
```

index.haml

```
1 %body
2   %h1
3     Hello World!
```

Now, let's start the application:

```
$ ruby helloworld.rb
```

After this, open the browser and point it to http://localhost:4567.

What did the code do?

You might have already guessed how this code works. We have added a new require line to helloworld.rb. This loads the haml gem. In the controller, we are returning a haml instead of a string.

Let's see line 5 once again:

```
5   haml :index
```

This is a ruby method call. The haml method has argument:index. The method will look for a file named index.haml in the views folder, generate the HTML from HAML, and return it to the client.

The following method will call the required file:

```
haml :<filename>
```

If the file does not exist in the views folder or if there are any syntax errors in HAML, then the application will throw an error.

Let's now see index.haml:

```
1 %body
2   %h1
3     Hello World!
```

We will see later that an HTML element can be defined by % in HAML and indented blocks can be used to define child elements. So, the preceding code will be interpreted as follows:

```
<body>
  <h1>
    Hello World!
  </h1>
</body>
```

To Sinatra or not to Sinatra?

Every framework has its own set of pros and cons. Sinatra is not the perfect framework for everything. Here are some of them.

Why Sinatra?

- You want to be flexible and choose your own gems and libraries. Unlike Rails, Sinatra lets the user choose whatever gems s/he wants to use.
- You want a higher performance. Sinatra is lightweight and does only the stuff that you want it to do.
- You want to make a completely modular application.
- You want to build an API.
- You want to learn Rails.
- You want to implement concurrency.

Why not Sinatra?

- You feel that Rails suits your project
- You have used Rails earlier and are comfortable with it
- You find that the conventions in Rails are good to work with

Other frameworks

Sinatra is not the only framework being used. Here are some more that you might have heard of:

- Zend for PHP
- Django for Python
- Rails and Merb for Ruby

- ASP.NET for .NET
- Catalyst for Perl
- Backbone.js for JavaScript
- Express for NodeJS

Summary

So, now that we have discussed what MVC is and how it is useful, you can understand how to write your application such that the responsibilities are clearly separated in the code. Additionally, if you are familiar with Ruby, you might have seen how easy it is to get started with Sinatra and build a web server in minutes.

Don't worry if you could not try out the codes in this chapter as we will be covering the same in detail soon. In the next chapter, we will be discussing the basic concepts of Ruby. We will be discussing enough for you to get started with Ruby and Sinatra, install Ruby and gems, and understand the data structures in Ruby. There will be a lot for you to explore that you will find really exciting when we go further with the book.

2
Introduction to Ruby

In this chapter, you will learn how to install Ruby and the basic built-in classes. This chapter will cover enough to get you started with Sinatra and make you comfortable with exploring more. This is not a complete guide to Ruby. If you have worked with any OOP language such as C++ or Java, this chapter will be a piece of cake for you.

Installation

Let's get into some action and install Ruby. If you are using Linux, Ruby can be installed using **Ruby Version Manager** (**RVM**) either system-wide or for a particular user. It can also be installed from the package manager. Using RVM simplifies managing multiple Ruby versions and gemsets. We will be using RVM to install Ruby for a single user.

On Windows, Ruby can be directly installed from the binary packages available. No rocket science.

Perform the following steps depending on your operating system.

For Linux users

If you are using Linux, you will need to install RVM first. This will create a .rvm folder in your home folder, which will have your rubies, gems, and gemsets. This is very convenient as you can just copy your .rvm folder and take your configurations along with you if you change your machine or Linux distribution:

1. Step 1: Install RVM:

   ```
   $ \curl -sSL https://get.rvm.io | bash -s stable
   ```

   As discussed, this will install RVM in your home folder.

2. Step 2: Install Ruby.

   After installation, you will need to load RVM in your shell session. Use the following code to load:

   ```
   $ source ~/.rvm/scripts/rvm
   ```

3. Now, we'll check whether RVM is configured properly or not:

   ```
   $ type rvm | head -n 1
   rvm is a function
   ```

4. You should see `rvm is a function` as the output. Once your RVM is ready, you need to know which Ruby you want to use. Type the following:

   ```
   $ rvm list known
   ```

5. This will list all the available versions of Ruby. Once you have decided which one to install, we can use the `rvm install` command. For our use case, we will use Ruby `2.0.0-p195`:

   ```
   $ rvm install 2.0.0-p195
   ```

This will install Ruby-2.0.0-p195 for your user. You might see the newer versions of Ruby by the time you read this and it is completely fine to go ahead with the rest of the book.

For Windows users

If you are using Windows, you can install Ruby using RubyInstaller. Go to the downloads section at http://www.rubyinstaller.org, download the binary of the Ruby version you want to install, and execute it. That's it and Ruby is installed.

You can use pik, which is similar to RVM but available only for Windows.

IRB

Interactive Ruby (IRB) is an interactive shell where you can try out your code or just play around. IRB comes in really handy to try out small pieces of code. For the rest of the chapter, you can try out the code examples in IRB or create files and execute them. In the examples, we will be doing both so that you can be comfortable using either.

Installation

IRB comes along with Ruby. So, installing Ruby will also install the correct irb.

Using IRB

Type `irb` on your command line to start the shell:

```
2.0.0-p195 :001 > puts "Hello World!"
Hello World!
 => nil
```

The `=> nil` that you see is the return value of the statement executed. So you don't need to worry about it much.

You can run any valid Ruby code in irb. Use it to play around with objects and find out what methods are available on them. Additionally, you must remember that everything in Ruby is an object.

Use `Object.methods` to get the list of methods available, for example:

```
2.0.0-p195 :002> "foo".methods
```

Let's now go through the Ruby basics and cover the various data types, control statements, classes, and objects one by one. This will give you a clear idea of how to start and enough space to discover as you proceed.

Ruby data types

Let's go through some of the data types in Ruby. You might be familiar with most of them.

Strings

Strings in Ruby are like strings in any other language. Though Ruby provides a lot of methods on the String object, for any string, you have a variety of handy methods such as `upcase`, `downcase`, `swapcase`, `capitalize`, `split`, `reverse`, `size`, `gsub`, and so on.

You might have guessed what these methods do. Use irb to try out these methods and other methods on the `String` object.

Numbers

Numbers comprise of `Integers` and `Floats`. Integers in Ruby are objects of the `Fixnum` class while floats are objects of the `Float` class.

Apart from the standard mathematical operators that you can apply on these objects, there are various other methods such as the following:

```
Fixnum - even?, odd?, to_f, to_s, times
Float - floor, ceiling, round, to_i, to_s
```

Use irb to find out what other methods the Fixnum and Float classes have.

Symbols

Symbols are lightweight objects in Ruby. Symbols can be used instead of strings in many places. As you know that everything in Ruby is an object, let's see this in irb:

```
2.0.0-p195 :001 > "foo".object_id
 => 16351980
2.0.0-p195 :002 > "foo".object_id
 => 16362580
2.0.0-p195 :003 > :foo.object_id
 => 535048
2.0.0-p195 :004 > :foo.object_id
 => 535048
```

So, we can see that for the same strings, Ruby will treat them as separate objects, while for the same symbols, it treats them as the same object.

Arrays

Arrays are ordered, integer-indexed collections of any object. In many languages, arrays cannot have elements of different types, but Ruby does not have this restriction, for example:

```
arr = [1, 2, 3]
arr2 = [1, 'Hello', 'World', [4, 5, 6]]
```

Both of these are perfectly valid arrays in Ruby.

An array's indices start from 0. Though Ruby supports negative indices, a negative index represents the *nth* last of the array:

```
arr[0] = 1, arr[1] = 2, arr[2] = 3, arr[-1] = 3, arr[-2] = 2, arr[-3]
= 1
```

The arr[-4] index and other lower indices are invalid.

Let's see some methods available on the objects of the Array class.

Array.each

Now, what we see here is a code-block:

```ruby
arr = [1, 2, 3]
arr.each do |e|
  puts e
end
```

In Ruby, code-blocks can be passed around like arguments. We will see more about code-blocks later in this chapter. For now, just consider them as simple blocks.

You can write this code in a text-file with the .rb extension or directly use irb:

```
2.0.0-p195 :001 > arr = [1, 2, 3]
 => [1, 2, 3]
2.0.0-p195 :002 > arr.each do |e|
2.0.0-p195 :003 >     puts e
2.0.0-p195 :004?>   end
1
2
3
 => [1, 2, 3]
```

You can write any other statement inside the code-block, which will be evaluated every time the block iterates. Note that the return value of the code is the original array.

Array.include

This method can be used to find the existence of an object in an array:

```
:005 > arr.include? 1
 => true
:006 > arr.include? 4
 => false
```

Array.map

This method iterates over each element and lets you map it with another value or object:

```
:007 >   arr.map do |e|
:008 >       e*2
:009?>   end
 => [2, 4, 6]
```

Now, the following method will not change the value of the original array:

```
:010 > arr = arr.map { |e| e*2 }
 => [2, 4, 6]
```

This will change the original method. Here, we also see another way of using code-blocks.

You can also use `map!` instead:

```
:011 > arr.map! { |e| e*2 }
 => [2, 4, 6]
```

Array.select

This method returns a subset of the array that matches the condition given which the code-block passed:

```
:012 >     arr.select {|e| e.odd?}
 => [1, 3]
:013 > arr.select {|e| e.even?}
 => [2]
```

Now you can play around with methods such as `pop`, `push`, `reverse`, `size`, `empty?`, and others on irb.

Hashes

Hashes are very similar to arrays except that you can use any object as an index (key) for a value, for example:

```
hash = {'foo' => 'bar'}
hash2 = {[1,2,3] => {}}
hash3 = {{}=>'hello'}
```

All three are valid hashes in Ruby. In the first one, the key is a string and so are the values. In the second, the key is an array and value is an empty hash, while in the third, the key is an empty hash and value is a string:

```
hash4 = {[] => 'string', 'hello' => {}}
```

The `hash4` object is also a perfectly valid hash. So basically, in Ruby, a hash is a collection of keys and values, where each key and each value should be a valid Ruby hash.

Let's check out some methods available to the Hash object.

Hash.each

This method iterates over each key-value pair of the hash and does the operation provided in the code-block passed:

```
:001 > hash = {:key1 => 'value1', :key2 => 2}
 => {:key1=>"value1", :key2=>2}
:002 > hash.each { |k, v| puts hash[k] }
value1
2
 => {:key1=>"value1", :key2=>2}
```

Hash.include?

This method can be used to find the existence of a key in a hash:

```
:003 > hash.include? :key1
 => true
:004 > hash.include? 'k'
 => false
```

Hash.keys

This method returns all the keys that exist in the given hash:

```
:005 > hash.keys
 => [:key1, :key2]
```

Hash.select

This selects elements from a hash matching the given condition:

```
:006 > hash.select {|k,v| hash[k] == 2}
 => {:key2=>2}
```

Now play around with hash in irb and find out methods such as `clear`, `delete`, `size`, and so on.

Code blocks

Code-blocks in Ruby are pieces of multiline code written in curly brackets or within a `do..end` block that can be passed around to methods such as parameters.

While discussing arrays, we saw the following:

```
arr.each do |e|
  puts e
end
```

Here, lets see what the preceding code will do:

```
do |e|
  puts e
end
```

This is a code-block which is passed as a parameter to the `arr.each` function.

Apart from passing code, code-blocks can be used to implement iterators and callbacks.

Classes and objects

Ruby is a multi-paradigm language and it supports object-oriented paradigms like any other OO language does. We can have modules, classes, methods, objects, inheritance, and so on.

Defining modules and classes

Like any other object-oriented language, we can define modules and classes in Ruby. A module is generally used to encapsulate one or more classes and improve readability. In the next few chapters, we will see how defining modules can improve the quality of the code:

```
module <module_name>
  class <class_name>
  end
end
```

For example, let's see the following code:

```
module Vehicle
  class Car
  end
end
```

Constructors

We can have constructor methods for the `Car` class:

```ruby
class Car
  def initialize(manufacturer, cost)
    @manufacturer = manufacturer
    @cost = cost
  end
end
```

The `def` function is used to define a method in Ruby.

Here, we have added `@` before the variable name. This denotes an instance variable. To define a class variable, we use `@@`.

Class methods and instance methods

Method names must begin with a lowercase letter. The name may end with a `?` if the method acts as a query and returns `true` or `false`:

```ruby
class Car
  def self.about
    puts "Class about cars."
  end

  def cost
    puts @cost
  end
end
```

To define a class method, we use `self` before the method name. We can also use the class name or `<<`:

```ruby
def self.about
  puts "Class about cars."
end

def Car.about
  puts "Class about cars."
end

def <<about
  puts "Class about cars."
end
```

All three are the same.

Defining methods

There are various options available to us when we are defining methods. So far, we have seen how to define class methods and instance methods. Now we will read about other options available, which can be used with both class and instance methods.

Methods with no arguments

We can use this type of definition when the method is not expecting any argument:

```
def method_name
  # code
end
```

Here, we can see that the method does not accept any arguments and if we pass arguments while calling the method, it will throw a wrong number of arguments error.

Methods with a fixed number of arguments

We can use this type of definition when the method is expecting a fixed number of argument(s):

```
def method_name arg1, arg2
  # code
end
```

The preceding method accepts exactly two arguments. Unlike many languages such as Java or C++, we do not need to define the data type of the argument.

While calling the method, we need to pass the correct number of arguments, otherwise it will throw a wrong number of arguments error.

Additionally, you do not need to specify parentheses while defining or calling methods:

```
def method_name (arg1, arg2)
  # code
end
```

This definition is exactly the same as the previous one.

Arguments with default values

We can use this type of definition when the method can have some optional arguments:

```
def method_name arg1, arg2='hello'
  # code
end
```

The preceding method also accepts exactly two arguments. If you specify only one argument, then the value of the second argument will be `hello` by default. Try this code in a Ruby file:

```
def foo a, b = 10
  puts a, b
end

foo 1, 2
```

Run the file from your command line and see the output:

1

2

As we have specified two arguments, the default value of b is not considered. Now, change the preceding code and pass only one argument:

```
def foo a, b = 10
  puts a, b
end

foo 1
```

Run the code and see the output:

```
1
10
```

As we have specified only one argument, the default value of b is considered (which is 10).

In many languages, the arguments with default values need to be defined at the end of the list:

```
def foo arg1, arg2, arg3 = value, arg4 = value
```

However, in Ruby, you can have the arguments with default values either in the beginning or at the end of the argument list:

```
def foo a, b = 10
```

Now lets see by ending style:

```
def foo a = 10, b
```

Both of the preceding definitions are correct.

However, you cannot have arguments with default values in the middle:

```
def method_name a = 1, b, c = 2
```

The preceding definition would be incorrect.

Now let's try something interesting. Write a file with the following code:

```
def foo a = 10, b = 11, c
  puts a, b, c
end


foo 1, 2
```

We know the output when we pass one argument and three arguments (note that passing zero or more than three arguments would throw an error, `wrong number of arguments`). However, which arguments will be assigned with which values when we pass two values?

Run this code and see the output:

```
1
11
2
```

This behavior can be confusing to some who are reading the code.

Methods with variable-length argument lists

There might be situations where you don't know the numbers of arguments you will need. Don't worry about this; achieving this is very simple:

```
def method_name arg1, arg2, *other_args
  # code
end
```

Here, `arg1` and `arg2` will be the required parameters and `*other_args` will take care of the rest of the argument lists. The `*other_args` will be an object of the `Array` class. Let's see an example code; create a new file or try it out in irb:

```
def foobar *all_args
  puts all_args.class
  puts all_args.length
```

```
end

foobar 1, 2, 3, 4, 5
```

Now run this code:

```
Array
5
```

So, we can see how easy it is to handle the various options that we get with arguments.

Private, protected, and public methods

In Ruby, you can manage the access controls of the methods by specifying one of the access specifiers. Let's know more about them:

- Public: Methods with public access can be called by anyone. The `initialize` method is always private.

- Protected: Methods with protected access can be called only by the objects of the class and its subclasses.

- Private: Methods with private access can be called only by the objects of the class:

  ```
  class Example
    # default is public
    def method1
      # code
    end

    private
    # all methods defined below this will be private
    def method2
      # code code code
    end

    protected
    # all methods defined below this will be protected
    def method3
      # more code
    end

    public
    # all methods defined below this will be public
    def method4
      # and just a little more of code
    end
  end
  ```

You can specify the access specifiers in any order. The methods defined after a particular specifier will have the appropriate access.

Control structures in Ruby

Ruby has various control structures, many of which you will be familiar with. A control structure executes statements until the condition is not false. Any value that is not nil or false is treated as true. For some of you who are comfortable with C++ or Java, you may sometimes find it confusing that 0 and empty string are not false.

if-elsif-else-end

The if-elsif-else-end control structure in Ruby is exactly the same as that in other programming languages:

```
if <condition>
  <statements>
elsif <condition>
  <statements>
else
  <statements>
end
```

Here is an example:

```
a = 1
b = 2
if a > b
  puts "The value of a is greater than the value of b"
elsif a < b
  puts "The value of a is less than the value of b"
else
  puts "The value of a is equal to the value of b"
end
```

Change the values of a and b to see how the control flows works.

unless..end

The unless method is equivalent to if not:

```
unless <condition>
  <statements>
end
```

Here is an example:

```
a = 1
b = 2
unless a == b
  puts "The value of a is not equal to the value of b"
end
```

You can use the optional `else` and nested conditions with the `unless..end` block as well.

Ternary operator

Ruby also has the classic ternary operator:

```
<condition> ? <truth> : <falsity>
```

Here is an example:

```
a = 1
b = 2
a > b ? puts a : puts b
```

Inline conditions

Sometimes, when the statement to be executed in a conditional block is just one line, it doesn't makes sense to write two additional lines for it. You can specify the condition in the same line for such cases. The following is an example:

```
puts "Hello World!" if a == 1
```

This will print `Hello World!` only if the value of `a` is `1`.

Similarly, you can have the following:

```
puts "Hello World!" unless a == 1
```

We can use it in a different way:

```
puts "Hello World!" if not a == 1
```

Case

The case control structure allows the execution of different statement groups based on different values of a given expression or variable:

```
case <expression>
when <value1>
   <statements>
when <value2>
   <statements>
when <value3>
   <statements>
else
   <statements>
end
```

Here is an example:

```
year = 2014
case
when year % 400 == 0
   puts "Leap year"
when year % 100 == 0
   puts "Not a leap year"
else year % 4 == 0
   puts "Leap year"
end
```

Operators

Apart from the common ==, <, <=, >=, > and !=, Ruby has a few other comparative operators:

```
<=>
```

This compares two objects and returns -1, 0, or +1.

Try the following in irb:

```
2.0.0-p195 :001 > 10 <=> 15
 => -1
```

The return value is -1.

eql?

The `eql?` function returns true if both the objects are of the same type and have the same value.

Try the following in irb:

```
2.0.0-p195 :002 > 1.eql? 1.0
 => false
```

equal?

The `equal?` function returns true if both the objects have the same object ID.

Try this in irb:

```
2.0.0-p195 :003 > "hello".equal? "hello"
 => false
2.0.0-p195 :004 > :hello.equal? :hello
 => true
```

Note how it returns `false` in the first comparison and `true` in the second.

Loops

Ruby has basic loop structures. You will find it very easy to understand them.

while-end

The while-end control structure is executed until the condition is true:

```
while <condition>
  <statements>
end
```

The statements are executed until the condition is false.

until-end

This loop structure is the opposite of the while-end structure:

```
until <condition>
  <statements>
end
```

The statements are executed until the statement is false.

Fixnum.times

This is similar to the `for` loop that you might have worked with in other languages:

```
Fixnum.times do
  <statements>
end
```

for..in

The `for..in` loop structure iterates over an object:

```
for <variable> in <object>
  <statements>
end
```

Here is an example:

```
for i in [1, 2, 3, 4, 5]
  puts i
end
```

Controlling the flow of iterations

It might sometimes be necessary to control the iterations in a loop structure for some conditions. Ruby provides three statements to control this flow:

- `break`: This breaks the loop and comes out without executing any statements further
- `redo`: This restarts the current iteration, skipping the execution of later statements
- `next`: This starts the next iteration of the loop, skipping the execution of later statements
- `restart`: This restarts the loop from the beginning

All these are generally used with conditions. Let's see an example:

```
for i in [1, 2, 3, 4, 5, 6 ]
  redo if i == 2
  next if i == 3
  break if i == 4
  retry if i == 5
  puts i
end
```

The preceding code shows the usage of all the four iteration controlling statements. Note that the preceding code will result in an infinite loop after the first iteration. The redo function is not useful in cases where the value of the iterator does not change even on redoing.

Even the `retry if i == 5` statement makes the code an infinite loop.

Exception handling

One of the more important tasks of writing code is handling exceptions. The exception handling block can be defined by the following structure:

```
begin
  # statements
rescue
  # handle error
else
  # statements to be executed if there are no errors
ensure
  # statements to be executed whether an error occurred or not
end
```

We can also use the `raise` statement to explicitly raise an exception.

This will be clearer by the following example:

```
begin
  for i in [1, 2, 3, 4, 5]
    raise if i == 4
    puts i
  end
rescue
  puts "Reached 4"
  next
else
  puts "No errors"
ensure
  puts "Iteration completed."
end
```

The output of the code will be as follows:

```
1
2
3
Reached 4
Iteration completed.
```

Summary

In this chapter, we discussed the fundamentals of Ruby. We saw how to install Ruby, and covered the various data types, defining classes and methods, loops, conditional execution, exceptional handling, and so on. Though this is not a complete reference to Ruby, the content of this chapter is enough to get you started with Ruby and Sinatra. It will help you explore more and innovate your code.

So, play around with various code snippets and use irb as it'll be of great help later. In the next chapter, we will start looking at Sinatra and its fundamentals.

3
Hello World

Now that we are confident with Ruby, let's get into action and start writing an application. Make sure that you have Ruby installed. We will get a basic skeleton app up and running and see how to structure the application.

In this chapter, we will discuss the following topics:

- A project that we will use to understand Sinatra
- The Bundler gem
- The file structure of the application
- Responsibilities of each file

Before we begin writing our application, let's write the **Hello World** application.

Getting started

We have seen the Hello World program in the first chapter:

```
1 require 'sinatra'
2
3 get '/' do
4   return 'Hello World!'
5 end
```

We have also discussed how this code works:

```
ruby helloworld.rb
```

Executing this from the command line will run the application and the server will listen to port 4567. If we point our browser to `http://localhost:4567/`, we can see the output as shown in the following screenshot:

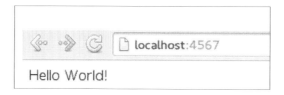

The application

To understand how to write a Sinatra application, we will take up a small project and discuss every part in detail, in this and the following chapters.

The idea

We shall make a ToDo app and use Sinatra and a lot of other libraries. The features of the app will be as follows:

- Each user can have multiple todo lists
- Each todo list will have multiple items
- Todo lists can be private, public, or shared with a group
- Items in each todo list can be assigned to a user or group

The modules that we will build are as follows:

- **Users**: This will manage users and groups
- **List**: This will manage the todo lists
- **Items**: This will manage the items for all the todo lists

Before we start writing the code, let's see what the file structure will be like, understand why each one of them is required, and learn about some new files.

The file structure

It is always good to keep certain files in certain folders for better readability. We can dump all the files in the `home` folder but that will make it difficult for us to manage the code:

```
.
├── app.rb
├── config.ru
├── Gemfile
├── lib
│   └── routes.rb
├── models
├── public
└── views
```

app.rb

This file is the base file that loads all the other files (`models`, `libs`, and so on) and starts the application. We can configure various settings of Sinatra here according to various deployment environments.

config.ru

The `config.ru` file is generally used when we need to deploy our application with different application servers, such as Passenger, Unicorn, or Heroku. It is also easy to maintain the different deployment environments using `config.ru`.

Gemfile

This is one of the interesting things that we can do with Ruby applications. As we know, we can use a variety of gems for different purposes. The gems are just pieces of code and are constantly updated. So, sometimes we need to use specific versions of gems to maintain the stability of our application.

We list all the gems that we are going to use for our application with their version. Before we discuss how to use this `Gemfile`, we shall talk about the gem `bundler` first.

Bundler

The gem bundler manages the installation of all the gems and their dependencies. Of course, we will need to install the gem bundler manually.

Gem install bundler

This will install the latest stable version of the bundler gem. Once we are done with this, we need to create a new file with the name Gemfile (yes, with a capital G) and add the gems that we will use. It is not necessary to add all the gems to the Gemfile before starting to write the application. We can add and remove gems as we require but after every change, we need to run the code.

Bundle install

This will make sure that all the required gems and their dependencies are installed. It will also create a file, `Gemfile.lock`. Make sure we do not edit this file. It contains all the gem and dependency information. So now we know why we should use Gemfile.

lib/routes.rb

This is a folder containing the `routes` file.

What is a route?

A route is the URL path for which the application serves a web page when requested. For example, when we type `http://www.example.com/`, the URL path is `/`; when we type `http://www.example.com/something/`, `/something/` is the URL path.

Now, we need to explicitly define all the routes for which we will be serving requests so that our application knows what to return. It is not important to have this file in the `lib` folder or to have this file at all. We can write the routes in the `app.rb` also.

Here are a few examples:

```
get '/' do
  # code
end

post '/something' do
  # code
end
```

Both of the preceding examples are valid routes. The `get` and `post` requests are the HTTP methods. The first code-block will be executed when a GET request is made on / and the second one, when a POST request is made on `/something`.

The only reason we are writing the routes in a separate file is to maintain clean code. The responsibility of each file will be clearly understood.

- **models/**: This folder contains all the files that define `model` of the application. When we write the models for our application, we will save it in this folder.

- **public/**: This folder contains all our css, JavaScript, and image files.

- **views/**: This folder contains all the files that define the views, such as HTML, HAML, or ERB files.

The code

Now we know what we want to build. We also have a rough idea of what our file structure will be. When we run the application, the `rackup` file that we load is `config.ru`. This file tells the server what environment to use and which file is the main application to load.

Before running the server, we need to write some minimal code. It includes writing three files:

- app.rb

- config.ru

- Gemfile

We can, of course, write these files in any order we want to, but we have to make sure that all three files have sufficient code for the application to work.

Let's start with `app.rb`.

app.rb

This is the file that config.ru loads when the application is executed. This file, in turn, loads all the other files that help it understand the available routes and underlying model:

```
1    require 'sinatra'
2
3    class Todo < Sinatra::Base
4      set :environment, ENV['RACK_ENV']
5
6      configure do
7      end
8
9          Dir[File.join(File.dirname(__FILE__),'models','*.rb')].
each { |model| require    model }
```

```
10      Dir[File.join(File.dirname(__FILE__),'lib','*.rb')].each {
|lib| load lib }
11
12    end
```

Breaking down the code

This defines our main application's class. This skeleton is enough to start the basic application. We inherit the `Base` class of the `Sinatra` module. Before starting the application, we might want to change some basic configuration settings such as logging, error display, user sessions, and so on. We handle all these configurations through The `configure` blocks. We might also need different configurations for different environments. For example, in development mode, we might want to see all the errors, but in production, we don't want the end user to see the error dump. So, we can define configurations for different environments.

The first step will be to set the application environment to the concerned one:

```
4      set :environment, ENV['RACK_ENV']
```

We will see later that we can have multiple configure blocks for multiple environments. This line reads the system environment variable `RACK_ENV` and sets the same environment for the application. When we discuss `config.ru`, we will see how to set `RACK_ENV` in the first place:

```
6      configure do
7      end
```

Here is how we define a configure block. Note that here we have not told the application the environment for which these configurations need to be applied. In such cases, this becomes the generic configuration for all the environments and this is generally the last configuration block. All the environment-specific configurations should be written before this block to avoid code overriding:

```
9    Dir[File.join(File.dirname(__FILE__),'models','*.rb')].each {
     |model| require model }
```

If we see the preceding file structure, we find that `models/` is a directory that contains the model files. We need to import all of these files to the application. We have kept all our model files in the `models/` folder:

```
Dir[File.join(File.dirname(__FILE__),'models','*.rb')]
```

This will return an array of files having an .rb extension in the models folder. Doing this avoids writing one required line for each file and modifying this file again and again:

```
10  Dir[File.join(File.dirname(__FILE__),'lib','*.rb')].each {
     |lib| load lib }
```

Similarly, we import all the files to the lib/ folder.

So, in short, app.rb configures our application according to the deployment environment and imports the model files and other library files before starting the application.

Now let's proceed to write our next file.

config.ru

The config.ru file is the rackup file of the application. This loads all the gems and app.rb. We generally pass this file as a parameter to the server:

```
1 require 'sinatra'
2 require 'bundler/setup'
3 Bundler.require
4
5 ENV["RACK_ENV"] = "development"
6
7 require File.join(File.dirname(__FILE__), 'app.rb')
8
9 Todo .start!
```

How the code works

Let's go through each of the lines:

```
1 require 'sinatra'
2 require 'bundler/setup'
```

The first two lines import the gems. This is exactly what we do in other languages. The gem 'sinatra' will include all the Sinatra classes and help in listening to requests, while the bundler gem will manage all the other gems. As we have discussed earlier, we will always use the bundler to manage our gems.

```
3 Bundler.require
```

This line of the code will check the Gemfile and make sure that all the gems available match the version and dependencies are met. This does NOT import all the gems as all the gems might not be needed in the memory at all times.

```
5 ENV["RACK_ENV"] = "development"
```

This code will set the system environment variable RACK_ENV to development. This will help the server know what configurations it needs to use. We will see later how to manage a single configuration file with different settings for different environments and use one particular set of configuration for the given environment.

> In case we use version control for our application, config.ru is not version-controlled. It has to be customized depending on whether our environment is development, staging, testing, or production. We might version-control a sample config.ru. We shall discuss this when we talk about deploying our application.

Next, we require the main application file:

```
7 require File.join(File.dirname(__FILE__), 'app.rb')
```

We can see that we have used the File class to include app.rb here:

```
File.dirname(__FILE__)
```

It is a convention to keep config.ru and app.rb in the same folder. It is a good habit to give the complete file path whenever we require a file to avoid breaking the code. So, this part of the code will return the path of the folder containing config.ru.

Now, we know that our main application file is in the same folder as config.ru, so we do:

```
File.join(File.dirname(__FILE__), 'app.rb')
```

This will return the complete file path of app.rb and line 7 will load the main application file in the memory. Now, all we need to do is execute app.rb to start the application:

```
9 Todo .start!
```

We see that the start! method is not defined by us in the Todo class in app.rb. This is inherited from the Sinatra::Base class. It starts the application and listens for incoming requests.

In short, config.ru checks the availability of all the gems and their dependencies, sets the environment variables, and starts the application.

The easiest file to write is the Gemfile. It has no complex code and logic. It just contains a list of gems and their version details.

Gemfile

In the Gemfile, we need to specify the source from which the gems will be downloaded and a list of the gems. So, let's write a Gemfile with the following lines:

```
1    source 'https://rubygems.org'
2    gem 'bundler', '1.6.0'
3    gem 'sinatra', '1.4.4'
```

The first line specifies the source; `https://rubygems.org` is a trusted place to download gems. It has a large collection of gems hosted. We can view this page and search for gems that we want to use, read the documentation, and select the exact version for our application. Generally, the latest stable version of bundler is used. So, we search the site for bundler and find out its version. We do the same for the Sinatra gem.

Starting the application

Earlier, we used to write the following on our command line to start our application:

```
ruby <filename>
```

For our current project, the main file is app.rb. As we also have a rackup file, we should start our application through that file:

```
ruby config.ru
```

This will execute config.ru and start the server. We will see something like this on our command line. This says that the Sinatra server is ready and listening for requests on port 4567 for the development deployment:

```
23:55 $ ruby app.rb
[2014-12-16 23:55:24] INFO  WEBrick 1.3.1
[2014-12-16 23:55:24] INFO  ruby 2.0.0 (2013-02-24) [x86_64-linux]
== Sinatra/1.4.4 has taken the stage on 4567 for development with backup from WEBrick
[2014-12-16 23:55:24] INFO  WEBrick::HTTPServer#start: pid=9577 port=4567
```

However, we have not defined our routes yet. So, all requests sent to this server would fail. We can define a few routes to check whether our application is running or not. So we edit the `lib/routes.rb` file and write this code:

```
get '/test' do
    return 'The application is running'
end
```

We know what this code will do, and if we restart the server and point our browser to `http://localhost:4567/test`, the web page should say: The application is running.

Features

Our next steps toward the development of this application will be defining models, writing routes, and designing views. We will not do this one at a time but rather, do all in parallel. This will finish one feature at a time.

Let's discuss the modules in detail and the feature set that we want. In the beginning of this chapter, we discussed that we will have three modules in our application:

- Users
- Lists
- Items

Users

The users module will manage all the users in our application. Our expectations from the user module can be as follows:

- It should allow the addition of new users
- It should allow the modification of existing users
- It should allow the management of permissions for todo lists

We will see in the next chapter how to exploit an ORM to define models but before that, we should know how our users table in the database will look. We can use MySQL or SQLite as the backend. So, the data types in the following tables will be as per these RDBMS.

The users table:

Field name	Data type	Length	Description
id	integer		This is the unique ID for every user; this is the primary key
username	string	15	This is a unique username
password	string	32	This is the MD5 hash of the password
name	string	30	This is the user's full name
created_at	date		This is the date the user joined

Lists

This module will manage all the todo lists. The following can be some expectations from the lists module:

- For a particular user, it should allow the creation of lists
- It should allow adding items to the list
- It should allow modifying items in the list
- It should allow changing permissions for a list
- It should show a log of actions on the list

We will have one table for all the lists, one for all the items, one for all the permissions, and one for all the logs for the list. This way, our tables will be normalized and it will very easy to write the code.

The lists table:

Field name	Data type	Length	Description
id	integer		This is the unique ID for every list; this is the primary key
name	string	20	This is the name of the list
shared_with	enum (private, shared, public)		This is the current sharing status of the list
created_at	date		This is the date the list was created

The items table:

Foreign keys - list id and the user id

Field name	Data type	Length	Description
id	integer		This is the unique ID for every item; this is the primary key
name	string	30	This is the name of the item
description	string	256	This is the description of the item
parent_list	integer		This is the foreign key from the list table that tells us to which this item belongs
created_by	integer		This is the foreign key from the user table that tells us who added this item
created_at	date		This is the date the list was created
updated_at	date		This is the date the list was updated

The permissions table:

Foreign keys - list id and the user id

Field name	Data type	Length	Description
id	integer		This is the unique ID for every permission; this is the primary key
list_id	integer		This is a foreign key from the list table
user_id	integer		This is a foreign key from the list table
permission_level	enum (read_only, read_write)		This defines the permission level for each user that the list is shared with
created_at	date		This is the date the permission was created
updated_at	date		This is the date when the permission was last updated

The logs table:

Foreign keys - list id and the user id

Field name	Data type	Length	Description
id	integer		This is the unique ID for every log; this is the primary key
list_id	integer		This is a foreign key from the list table that defines which list the log is for

Field name	Data type	Length	Description
user_id	integer		This is a foreign key from the user table that defines which user the log is for
log	string	256	This is the log that describes the action
created_at	date		This is the date the log was recorded on

Object Relationship Mapper

While discussing the project, we talked about **Object Relationship Mapper (ORM)**. ORMs are libraries that act as a database wrapper for the programmer. It provides you with methods to communicate with the backend and can manage multiple types of data stores. So, in case we want to switch our data store, we will have to change just one line in the configuration part of the ORM and the rest of the code will remain the same.

This also makes the code cleaner and more readable and reliable. Though it makes the application a bit slower, the trade-off is worth it.

So, now that we know how our table structure will be, we have a better and clearer idea of what our application will be like. We will be discussing how to manage our backend using an ORM in the next chapter. It will give us a better idea as to why we are using one and not talking to the data store directly.

If you notice the expectations of each module, you might guess what our routes will be like.

We will discuss later how to write routes effectively and use advanced Sinatra methods and features to make the workflow simple.

Designing views

Now that we have a clear understanding of the features that we want to implement for our application, we should also talk about the views or user interfaces that we will have to design.

We can use HTML directly and create forms and user interfaces for the application. We can also write our own CSS to design the UI. As we are using Ruby, we should exploit any feature that it provides in order to improve our efficiency.

In the first chapter, we discussed HAML. For our project, we will be using HAML to design our views. HAML is a lightweight templating language over HTML and is very easy to understand and implement. Ruby interprets HAML and generates HTML and then the browser renders it.

It is also important to make our user interfaces look good. Just using HTML is not enough as it does not have any designing capability. We will have to design using CSS. Now, if we start to write our own CSS code from scratch, it will take a lot of time. So, we will use some other freely available CSS framework such as Twitter Bootstrap (http://getbootstrap.com/). Bootstrap is very simple to understand and implement and it makes a great UI. We can customize it as per our needs if required.

We will design the following interfaces:

- The User Login page
- The User Registration page
- The User Profile page
- The Available Lists page
- The New Todo List page
- The Edit Todo List page

Summary

In this chapter, we discussed an idea that we will work on and the structure of the application. In the next few chapters, we will be discussing in detail how to write the routes, views, models, controllers, and so on as well as designing the whole application.

Making a complete application will help you get a clear idea on how to structure a Sinatra application. The next few chapters will be a combination of discussion and code implementation. We will start off with implementing the backend for our application where we will connect to a database using an ORM. We will read more on ORMs and how to use them with ruby in the next chapter.

4
Modeling the Backend

In the previous chapter, we discussed the structure of the ToDo application that we will architect. We discussed the structure of the tables in the backend, responsibilities of each module, and views that we will design.

In this chapter, we will discuss the following topics:

- What Object-relational mapping is
- When and why should ORM be used
- How to use ORM for our application

What is Object-relational mapping

For most of the applications that one builds, the choice of the backend application is very important. One may choose any of the SQL-based DBMS such as MySQL, MSSQL, and SQLite or NoSQL-based systems such as MongoDB. For our application, a SQL-based DBMS will work well and we can choose either SQLite or MySQL as they do not require any licenses to use.

In the model of our application, we can directly communicate with the database by writing SQL statements, or we could use an ORM.

When to use an ORM

Using an ORM has a lot of benefits over using standard SQL directly. Let's discuss some of them:

1. **Quick development**: One needs to create tables manually and manage them when using SQL directly. Using an ORM reduces all such overheads.

We can define classes that correspond to the table structure and every time we restart the application, the database is updated.

2. **Handling errors and transactions**: Instead of writing SQL statements to manage transactions and handle errors, we can write simple Ruby code to do the same.

3. **Independent of the DBMS**: ORMs are independent of the DBMS used. We can use the exact same code to communicate with any of the DBMS. We will just need to specify it while defining the connection and everything else will be taken care of by the underlying library.

So, in our case, using an ORM will be a lot of help. We will be using `Sequel` to help us with our backend needs.

Use the following code to install `sequel`:

```
gem install sequel
```

This will install the sequel and other dependent gems. Our next step will be to define migrations and models. In the previous chapter, we read about the various tables that we will need. We will see each model one by one and understand how to use Sequel to define them.

How to define migrations

In Sequel, we need to define `migrations` to create tables. Migration is a systematic procedure to change the schema of our database from one version to another. So, in our case, we will have numbered files (001, 002, ...) representing a new version. Sequel handles the migration files automatically and always checks for the newest file.

The users table

Currently, our database is empty and has no tables in it. The first schema change will be the first migration. So, let's write a `001_create_users_table.rb` file in the `db/migrations/` folder. Note that the filename can be anything as long as it starts with the proper number. We can also have `1_some_file_name`. The leading zeros are not mandatory. Also, the first migration is numbered 1 and not 0.

File: `001_create_users_table.rb`:

```
1    Sequel.migration do
2      change do
3        create_table :users do
4          primary_key :id
```

```
   5            String :name, :unique => true, :length => 32, :null =>
false
   6            String :password, :length => 32, :null => false
   7            DateTime :created_at
   8          end
   9        end
  10      end
```

Let's see the file line by line:

Line 1: `Sequel.migration do` defines a migration block that executes on a change.

Line 2: `change do` defines a change.

Line 3: `create_table :users do` will create a table named `users`.

Line 4: `primary_key :id` will create a attribute named `id` that will be the primary key.

Line 5: `String :name, :unique => true, :length => 32, :null => false` will define an attribute of a `string` type named `name`. The `:unique => true` constraint means that the values for the attribute should be `unique` and `:null => false` means that the value cannot be `null`.

Line 6: `String :password, :length => 32, :null => false` will create an attribute named `password`.

Line 7: `DateTime :created_at` will create an attribute named `created_at` of the `datetime` data type.

In MySQL, `String` will create a `varchar` type attribute and `DateTime` will create a `timestamp` type attribute.

After defining all the migrations, we will execute them to see the changes.

The lists table

Defining the list model will be the second change in our database schema and hence, we create a `002_create_list_table.rb` file:

```
   1    Sequel.migration do
   2      change do
   3        create_table :lists do
   4          primary_key :id
   5          String :name, :length => 32, :null => false
   6          column :shared_with, 'enum("private", "shared",
             "public")', :null => false, :default => 'private'
```

```
 7          DateTime :created_at
 8        end
 9      end
10    end
```

In line 6, we see a new way to create an attribute. We have used the `column` keyword. We can either use a data type such as `String`, `Integer`, or `DateTime` or, if we want to define some other type of attribute, we can use the `column` keyword. The `column` keyword can be used to define any attribute.

So the following code is perfectly fine:

```
column :name, :string
```

The items table

We know what to do next. The `003_create_items_table.rb` file will look as follows:

```
 1    Sequel.migration do
 2      change do
 3        create_table :items do
 4          primary_key :id
 5          String :name, :length => 128, :null => false
 6          String :description, :length => 256
 7          foreign_key :user_id, :users, :null => false
 8          foreign_key :list_id, :lists, :null => false
 9          DateTime :created_at
10          DateTime :updated_at
11        end
12      end
13    end
```

Here we see a new way to define attributes. In lines 7 and 8, we have used the concept of foreign keys. The `user_id` and `list_id` attributes are foreign keys from the users and lists tables respectively.

The permissions table

Let's create a `004_create_permissions_table.rb` file to define the permissions table:

```
 1    Sequel.migration do
 2      change do
 3        create_table :permissions do
 4          foreign_key :user_id, :users, :null => false
```

```
5          foreign_key :list_id, :lists, :null => false
6          column :permission_level, 'enum("read_only",
           "read_write")', :null => false
7          DateTime :created_at
8          DateTime :updated_at
9          primary_key [:user_id, :list_id], :name =>
           :permissions_pk
10       end
11     end
12   end
```

We haven't done anything new here. This migration will create the permissions table.

The logs table

This will be the last migration file, `005_create_logs_table.rb`:

```
1    Sequel.migration do
2      change do
3        create_table :logs do
4          primary_key :id
5          foreign_key :user_id, :users, :null => false
6          foreign_key :list_id, :lists, :null => false
7          String :log_line, :length => 256, :null => false
8          DateTime :created_at
9        end
10     end
11   end
```

We are now done with defining the structure of the tables. These migrations will be used just to create tables. However, to access the data as objects in our application, we need to define the Sequel models with the proper relationship. So, let's go ahead and define the models.

Let's understand the structure of our application:

1. There will be many users and many lists

2. Each list will have many items and each item will belong to exactly one list

3. Each user can have permissions to many lists and each list can have permissions for many users

4. Each user can add many items and each item will be added by exactly one user

Now, we will just need to define these relationships in our models.

How to define models

Migrations are not detected by the application. The application understands models. The models will have relationships defined. When we use Sequel, we get a lot of methods to access our data store as objects. Let's now define our models.

The User model

The user model will have the following properties:

1. Each user can add many items

2. Each user can have permission to many lists

3. Each user can have many logs

The file will be `model/user.rb`:

```
1    require 'sequel'
2
3    class User < Sequel::Model
4      set_primary_key :id
5
6      one_to_many :items
7      one_to_many :permissions
8      one_to_many :logs
9    end
```

Let's understand each line one by one:

- Line 3: `class User < Sequel::Model` tells the application to inherit the `Model` class of the `Sequel` module

- Line 4: `set_primary_key :id` defines the primary key for the `User` model

- Line 6: `one_to_many :items` means that one user can have many items and each item will correspond to exactly one user

- Line 7: `one_to_many :permissions` means that one user can have many permissions and each permission will correspond to exactly one user

- Line 8: `one_to_many :logs` means that one user can have many logs and each log will correspond to exactly one user

Our next file will be for the List model.

The List model

The list model will have the following properties:

1. Each list can have many items
2. Each list can have permission by many users
3. Each list can have many logs

The file will be `models/list.rb`:

```
1    require 'sequel'
2
3    class List < Sequel::Model
4      set_primary_key :id
5
6      one_to_many :items
7      one_to_many :permissions
8      one_to_many :logs
9    end
```

Let's understand the code line by line:

- Line 3: This is the same as the previous model, which means that the List model will inherit the `Model` class of the `Sequel` module.

- Line 4: This defines the primary key.

- Line 6: `one_to_many :items` means that each list will have many items and every item will correspond to exactly one list.

- Line 7: `one_to_many :permissions` is similar to line 5 in the `User` model. It means that one list can have many permissions and each permission will correspond to exactly one user.

- Line 8: This is similar to line 8 in the `User` model, which means that each list can have many logs and each log will correspond to exactly one list.

To make our code readable, we should define the `Item` model in the same file. Note that we can define all the models in the same file. The application doesn't care about the number of files. However, for the sake of clarity, we will define related models in one file.

So, in the same `list.rb`, we define the `Item` model:

```
1    require 'sequel'
2
3    class List < Sequel::Model
4      set_primary_key :id
```

```
 5
 6      one_to_many :items
 7      one_to_many :permissions
 8      one_to_many :logs
 9    end
10
11    class Item < Sequel::Model
12      set_primary_key :id
13
14      many_to_one :user
15      many_to_one :list
16    end
```

Let's understand the code line by line:

- Line 14: `many_to_one :user` is the inverse of `one_to_many`. It means that many items can correspond to one user, but one item cannot correspond to many users.

- Line 15: `many_to_one :list` means that many items can correspond to one list but one item cannot correspond to many lists.

Let's go ahead and define the `Permission` model.

Permission Model

The `Permission` model will now just need to define the relationship between permissions and users and permissions and lists.

The file will be `model/permission.rb`:

```
1    require 'sequel'
2
3    class Permission < Sequel::Model
4      many_to_one :user
5      many_to_one :list
6    end
```

Let's understand the code line by line:

- Line 4: `many_to_one :user` means that each permission will correspond to exactly one user

- Line 5: `many_to_one :list` means that each permission will correspond to exactly one list

The Log model

Similar to the permission model, the log model defines the relationship between logs and users and logs and lists:

- Each user can have logs for many lists
- Each list can have logs for many users

The file will be `model/log.rb`:

```
1    require 'sequel'
2
3    class Log < Sequel::Model
4      set_primary_key :id
5
6      many_to_one :user
7      many_to_one :list
8    end
```

The explanation of the preceding code is given as follows:

- Line 4: `many_to_one :user` means that each log will correspond to exactly one user
- Line 5: `many_to_one :list` means that each log will correspond to exactly one list

Before we go deeper, let's recap what we have done so far:

- We have defined sequential migrations that will create tables in the database in MySQL
- We have defined models so that our application can access these tables as objects and we can take advantage of the various methods that `Sequel::Model` provides as an ORM

How to run migrations

Now we have defined all our migrations. To change the schema of our database, we need to execute all of them. We have already installed the `sequel` gem and we have five migration files in the `db/migrations` folder.

So, for sequel to create the tables, we need to create a database first. In the command prompt, we type the following command:

```
mysql -u root -p
```

This will open the MySQL shell by entering the password for the `root` user. You can also use `mysql -u user -p` if you want to use a different user for the application:

```
mysql> create database todo;
```

This will create a database named `todo`. Now we need to execute the migration files to populate the tables.

Now, close the MySQL console and run the following command on the console of your operating system's application folder to execute the migrations:

```
sequel -m db/migrations/ mysql://root:root@localhost/todo
```

This command is of the following format:

```
sequel -m path/to/migrations mysql://user:password@host/database
```

If you have created the database with a different user, then replace the user and password with proper values.

The command will not print anything on the console.

We will now check whether our tables have been populated perfectly or not. Open the MySQL console, `mysql -u root -p`, and use `describe` to check each table one by one.

We will see the list of tables that exists in our database using the following commands:

```
mysql> use todo;
Database changed
mysql> show tables;
+----------------+
| Tables_in_todo |
+----------------+
| items          |
| lists          |
| logs           |
| permissions    |
| schema_info    |
| users          |
+----------------+
6 rows in set (0.00 sec)
```

Fig 4-1: List of tables

The first table that we will check is the `users` table:

```
mysql> desc users;
+------------+--------------+------+-----+---------+----------------+
| Field      | Type         | Null | Key | Default | Extra          |
+------------+--------------+------+-----+---------+----------------+
| id         | int(11)      | NO   | PRI | NULL    | auto_increment |
| name       | varchar(255) | NO   | UNI | NULL    |                |
| password   | varchar(255) | NO   |     | NULL    |                |
| created_at | datetime     | YES  |     | NULL    |                |
+------------+--------------+------+-----+---------+----------------+
4 rows in set (0.00 sec)
```

Fig 4-2: Structure of the users table

We can see that the `users` table is as expected. So now let's see the `lists` table:

```
mysql> desc lists;
+-------------+---------------------------------+------+-----+---------+----------------+
| Field       | Type                            | Null | Key | Default | Extra          |
+-------------+---------------------------------+------+-----+---------+----------------+
| id          | int(11)                         | NO   | PRI | NULL    | auto_increment |
| name        | varchar(255)                    | NO   |     | NULL    |                |
| shared_with | enum('private','shared','public') | NO |   | private |                |
| created_at  | datetime                        | YES  |     | NULL    |                |
+-------------+---------------------------------+------+-----+---------+----------------+
4 rows in set (0.01 sec)
```

Fig 4-3: Structure of the lists table

The lists table also has the properties that we have defined in our migrations. Let's now see the items table and check whether the foreign key constraints from the users and lists are fine or not:

```
mysql> desc items;
+-------------+--------------+------+-----+---------+----------------+
| Field       | Type         | Null | Key | Default | Extra          |
+-------------+--------------+------+-----+---------+----------------+
| id          | int(11)      | NO   | PRI | NULL    | auto_increment |
| name        | varchar(255) | NO   |     | NULL    |                |
| description | varchar(255) | YES  |     | NULL    |                |
| user_id     | int(11)      | YES  | MUL | NULL    |                |
| list_id     | int(11)      | YES  | MUL | NULL    |                |
| created_at  | datetime     | YES  |     | NULL    |                |
| updated_at  | datetime     | YES  |     | NULL    |                |
+-------------+--------------+------+-----+---------+----------------+
7 rows in set (0.00 sec)
```

Fig 4-4: Structure of the items table

The foreign key constraints appear to be perfect. Let's go through the structure of the `permissions` table and see if the `permission_level enums` are fine or not:

```
mysql> desc permissions;
+------------------+-------------------------------------+------+-----+---------+-------+
| Field            | Type                                | Null | Key | Default | Extra |
+------------------+-------------------------------------+------+-----+---------+-------+
| user_id          | int(11)                             | NO   | PRI | 0       |       |
| list_id          | int(11)                             | NO   | PRI | 0       |       |
| permission_level | enum('read_only','read_write')      | NO   |     | NULL    |       |
| created_at       | datetime                            | YES  |     | NULL    |       |
| updated_at       | datetime                            | YES  |     | NULL    |       |
+------------------+-------------------------------------+------+-----+---------+-------+
5 rows in set (0.00 sec)
```

Fig 4-5: Structure of the permissions table

So the `permissions` table also looks good. Just to confirm, we will also see the `logs` table once:

```
mysql> desc logs;
+------------+--------------+------+-----+---------+----------------+
| Field      | Type         | Null | Key | Default | Extra          |
+------------+--------------+------+-----+---------+----------------+
| id         | int(11)      | NO   | PRI | NULL    | auto_increment |
| user_id    | int(11)      | YES  | MUL | NULL    |                |
| list_id    | int(11)      | YES  | MUL | NULL    |                |
| log_line   | varchar(255) | NO   |     | NULL    |                |
| created_at | datetime     | YES  |     | NULL    |                |
+------------+--------------+------+-----+---------+----------------+
5 rows in set (0.01 sec)
```

Fig 4-6: Structure of the logs table

So, we can see that our database schema is ready as we want it to be. We can now write our application, which will interact with MySQL using Sequel. Before we do this, let's discuss the responsibilities of each model so that we know what methods we have to define.

What are the responsibilites of the models?

The application will pass on various requests to the models and hence the models should be ready to handle them. Let's take a look at what each model's responsibilities will be. We will also see what are the corresponding methods that Sequel provides for our ease.

The User model

The `User` model will be taking care of all the actions possible on a user. The responsibilities will be as follows:

- It should be able to create a new user.

  We can use the `create` method on the `User` model. This `create` method is defined in `Sequel::Model` and we can directly use it by passing the required values:

  ```
  User.create(name:'user1', password:'password')
  ```

  This method will create a user in the `users` table. If you remember, we have added a `unique` constraint to the `name` attribute. This will ensure that we will not have two users with the same name.

- It should be able to check the username and password on login.

  We can use the `find` method on the `User` model. This `create` method is defined in `Sequel::Model` and we can directly use it by passing the required values:

  ```
  User.find(name:'user1', password:'password')
  ```

  The `find` method returns all the records that match the condition. In our case, the `name` is unique and hence this method will return only one record if `name` and `password` are correct. It will return `nil` otherwise.

- It should be able to show the permission that a user has on lists.

  This is a very interesting case. The permissions for a user on a list are stored in the `permissions` table. However, in our `User` model, we have defined a `one_to_many` relationship with permissions. This will add a method named `permissions` to the `User` model, which will return all the records from the `permissions` table where the `user_id` attribute matches `id` of the user:

  ```
  user = User.create(name:'user1', password:'password')
  user.permissions
  ```

  This will return all the permissions for the `'user1'` user. We can also filter our search by passing the `permission_level` attribute.

To find the lists on which the user has `'read_write'` permission, we can use the following method:

```
user.permissions(permission_level:'read_write')
```

Similarly, the following method will return the records where the user has read_only permission:

```
user.permissions(permission_level:'read_only')
```

It should be able to show the logs that the user has generated from his actions on various lists.

Logs are similar to permissions, as we seen previously. So, to fetch all the logs for the 'user1' user, we can use the logs method.

The following method call will return all the logs generated for 'user1':

```
user.logs
```

So, we can see that using an ORM has made everything so simple. By providing us with all the methods that we need to, we have no need to write a single SQL statement or complex Ruby methods. We can directly call the methods generated by Sequel for all our actions.

We will now see the responsibilities of other models and the methods that Sequel provides. It will be very easy for you to guess the methods by now.

The List model

The List Model will be taking care of all the actions possible on a list. The responsibilities will be as follows:

- It should be able to create a new list.

  The create method can be used exactly in the way we used it in the User model:

  ```
  List.create(name:'list'1)
  ```

- It should be able to edit the name of a list.

  As discussed earlier, Sequel will provide us with methods to access each and every valid attribute of a model. So, to access the name attribute, the method will be name. Let's say that we have a list named 'list1':

  ```
  list = List.create(name:'list1')
  ```

  The list.name will return the name of the list. We can change the name using the following command:

  ```
  list.name = 'new name'
  list.save
  ```

What we see here is a common example of getter and setter methods that most of the programming languages provide. The save method is used to write the changes to the database:

- It should be able to delete a list.

  The delete method will remove the list from the database. Note that this is not reversible.

  ```
  list.delete
  ```

- It should allow adding permissions for a list.

  We have seen previously in the User model that Sequel has provided us with a permissions method. It has also provided a method named add_permission. This method expects a User object and the value for permission_level. So, if we have a object user for 'user1', we can use the following method to add permissions for a user:

  ```
  list.add_permission(user:user, permission_level:'read_write')
  ```

  This will add a record to the permissions table.

- It should be able to fetch a list.

  The same find method will be used here:

  ```
  List.find(name:'list1')
  ```

- It should allow adding items to a list.

  We can add items to the list in exactly the same way we add permissions. Note that in our application, we expect every item to correspond to a user. So, the add_item method expects a user too.:

  ```
  list.add_items(name:'item1_1', user:user)
  ```

- It should allow removing items from a list.

  We use the remove_item method to remove an item from the list:

  ```
  item = list.add_items(name:'item1_1', user:user)
  list.remove_item(item)
  ```

  Here, we can see that Sequel has provided us with a method to remove the item that has a many_to_one relationship with a list. We also have a remove_all_items method that removes all the items from the given list.

- It should allow adding permissions for a list.

  Similar to the add_permission method, we have an add_log method;

  ```
  list.add_log(user:user, log_line:'user1 has created the list.')
  ```

  This will add a record to the logs table.

The Item model

The `Item` model will be taking care of all the actions possible on an item. The responsibilities will be as follows:

- It should allow adding a new item to a particular list.

  This is done through the List model, though we can use `Item.create` to add a new item:

  ```
  Item.create(name:'item1', list:list, user:user)
  ```

  Here, `list:list` means that the value of the `list_id` field in the `items` table should refer to `id` of the `list` object that we have created earlier.

- It should allow editing an item.

  We created an item earlier using `item = list.add_items(name:'item1_1', user:user)`. This `item` object will have getter and setter methods, as seen previously. So, the following code can be used to edit the item:

  ```
  item.name = 'new item name'
  item.save
  ```

- It should allow deleting an item.

  Again, this should be done through the `list` model but we can also use the `delete` method on the `item` object:

  ```
  item.delete
  ```

The Permission model

The `Pemission` model will be taking care of all the actions possible on a permission. The responsibilities will be as follows:

All the permissions will be handled directly from the `List` model. So, this model will have no user-defined methods, though we can use the `find` method to search for permissions on a list for a user.

The Log model

All the logs will be handled directly from the `List` model. So, this model will have no user-defined methods.

Summary

In this chapter, we discussed how to design a backend and what the models for our application will look like. We have also seen how using an ORM eases our life. The ORM that we used was Sequel, and with the help of migrations, we can easily manage the database schema.

In the next chapter, we will write our Sinatra application, integrate the models into it, and see how the requests will be handled.

5
Handling HTTP Requests

In the previous chapter, we discussed the design of our database and how to use models and migrations efficiently. Now we know what we should take as input from the user and how to save it.

In this chapter, we will discuss the following topics:

- How to write an application that will listen for requests
- How to pass the requests to the model
- How to write methods in the models to process the requests

Understanding the application file – app.rb

We require a web server that will receive requests from the user and process them. The web server will pass the request to the application, which will check what kind of request it is and process accordingly. When we execute our Sinatra application, it starts a web server that listens for requests on a particular port.

If you recall the application file structure that we had discussed in *Chapter 3*, *Hello World*, you will find a file named app.rb. This file will be our main application file that will load all the models and handle all the requests.

The main application file loads all the Ruby gems, connects to the database, and loads all the models. It also manages requests for all the defined routes. A route is a valid HTTP request that the given application can understand and process.

Writing the application file is very simple. So, let's start it right away!

Writing app.rb

As discussed previously, the `app.rb` file that we will write should load all the gems and models.

Lets see the contents of file `app.rb`:

```
1    require 'sinatra'
2    require 'sequel'
3
4    class Todo < Sinatra::Application
5      configure do
6        DB = Sequel.connect("mysql://root:root@localhost/todo")
7
8        Dir[File.join(File.dirname(__FILE__),'models','*.rb')].
         each { |model| require model }
9      end
10   end
```

Let's go through this file line by line:

- Lines 1-2: These load the necessary gems, namely, `sinatra` and `sequel`. Sinatra is the main gem required to run the application and sequel is required to communicate with the database.

- Line 4: This defines a `Todo` class that extends the `Application` class of the `Sinatra` module. This loads all the methods from the `Application` class to the `Todo` class.

- Lines 5-9: This defines a configuration block that creates a connection with the database (line 6) and also loads all the models in the application's memory (line 8).

- Line 8: This loops over the `models` folder and loads all the files with `.rb` as the extension.

Our application needs these ten lines only. To test if everything is correct or not, we can execute this file on the command prompt by writing the following command:

```
ruby app.rb
```

We will get an output similar to the following:

```
[2014-09-21 23:10:26] INFO  WEBrick 1.3.1
[2014-09-21 23:10:26] INFO  ruby 2.0.0 (2013-02-24) [x86_64-linux]
== Sinatra/1.4.4 has taken the stage on 4567 for development with
backup from WEBrick
[2014-09-21 23:10:26] INFO  WEBrick::HTTPServer#start: pid=3549
port=4567
```

This means that the application is ready to accept requests on port 4567. Let's try by sending a request to the application.

Open up a web browser and type the following in the address bar:

```
http://localhost:4567/
```

You should see an error message from Sinatra, as shown in the following screenshot:

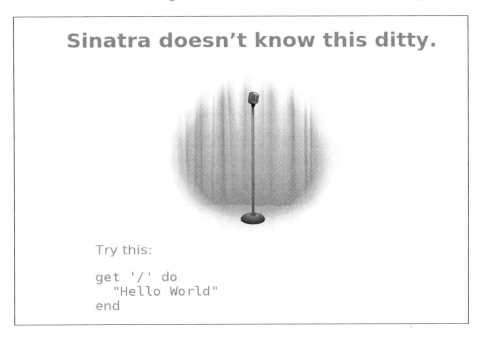

This means that our application is running perfectly fine. The error occurs because we haven't defined the valid routes.

Writing routes for the responsibilities of the application

So our next step will be defining the valid routes for our application. Let's discuss the responsibilities of our application:

- Showing a page for all the existing lists
- Showing a page to create a new list
- Saving a new list
- Deleting a list

- Showing a page to edit a list
- Updating a list
- Changing permissions on a list

Let's write the routes for each of these responsibilities in the following sections.

Showing a page for all the existing lists

This will load all the available lists from the database and a page that will show them. The route is defined by setting the URL path and defining the processing code. For example, in http://www.example.com/test/, the URL path is '/test/'; similarly, in http://www.example.com, the URL path is '/'. The trailing '/' is optional and so we need to handle this in our routes.

Now, we continue writing in app.rb:

```
1    require 'sinatra'
2    require 'sequel'
3
4    class Todo < Sinatra::Application
5      configure do
6        DB = Sequel.connect("mysql://root:root@localhost/todo")
7
8        Dir[File.join(File.dirname(__FILE__),'models','*.rb')].
           each { |model| require model }
9      end
10   end
11
12   get '/?' do
13     all_lists = List.all
14   end
```

Let's discuss the last three lines that we have added:

- Line 12: This defines a block. The 'get' method specifies that the request should be an HTTP GET request, '/?' specifies that the URL path should be '/', and '?' is a regex for 0 or 1 occurrence of '/'. Hence, both http://localhost:4567 and http://localhost:4567/ will mean the same.

- Line 13: The all method on the List class will select all the lists available in the database.

We will discuss the designing of HTML pages in the next chapter.

Showing a page to create a new list

We will have a view to create a new list. The view will be shown when the user makes a GET request on '/new/?'. The route definition will be written as shown in lines 16-18 of the following code:

```
12    get '/?' do
13      all_lists =  List.all
14    end
15
16    get '/new/?' do
17      # show create list paqe
18    end
```

We have not written the code to show the view but the route definition will not change. All the requests to '/new/?' will be handled here.

Handling the saving of a new list

The user will send the list form to the server using POST. We will need a valid route to handle this:

```
16    get '/new/?' do
17      # show create list page
18    end
19
20    post '/new/?' do
21      # save the list
22    end
```

Lines 20-22 define a block that will handle a POST request to save the list.

Showing a page to edit a list

Every list has a numeric primary key. To edit a list, the application will need to know this id in order to load the list data. Here is the code:

```
20    post '/new/?' do
21      # save the list
22    end
23
24    get '/edit/:id/?' do
25      # check user permission and show the edit page
26    end
```

If we look at line 24, we added `'/:id'` to the route itself. This will handle requests like `'/edit/1'` and we can access the value of `id`.

Handling the updating of a list

Similar to saving a new list, we have to handle the updating of an existing list. Here is the code:

```
24    get '/edit/:id/?' do
25      # check user permission and show the edit page
26    end
27
28    post '/edit/?' do
29      # update the list
30    end
```

Here, we do not require the `id` to be in the URL as the POST data will have it.

Handling the changing of permissions on a list

To change the permissions on a list, we need to handle the request. The following is the code:

```
28    post '/edit/?' do
29      # update the list
30    end
31
32    post '/permission/?' do
33      # update permission
34    end
```

Showing a page for signup

This will just return a view showing a signup form similar to the `create` list. Here is the code for it:

```
32    post '/permission/?' do
33      # update permission
34    end
35
36    get '/signup/?' do
37      # show signup form
38    end
```

Saving the new user data

Every time we show a form, we will have a corresponding POST request and we will need a route to handle this. You can do this as follows:

```
36    get '/signup/?' do
37      # show signup form
38    end
39
40    post '/signup/?' do
41      # save the user data
42    end
```

Showing a page for login

Again, this is a similar GET request to show a login form:

```
40    post '/signup/?' do
41      # save the user data
42    end
43
44    get '/login/?' do
45      # show a login page
46    end
```

Handling user login

The route defined in lines 48-50 will validate the user credentials. Here is the code:

```
44    get '/login/?' do
45      # show a login page
46    end
47
48    post '/login/?' do
49      # validate user credentials
50    end
```

Now we have the skeleton of the application with us. All the valid routes are known and we just need to send the data and design the views.

Sending the data and designing the views

We can divide the routes based on the type of HTTP requests that they handle (GET and POST). For all the GET requests, we might fetch some data from the backend and show an HTML page, and for all the POST requests, we will call a model method and return to the same HTML page. So, for now, we will just write the code to call an HTML page and design the actual pages later on.

To design the pages, we will use a templating engine called HAML. HAML is a ruby gem that makes it easier to write HTML codes. To make sure that our application doesn't throw any errors, we will install the HAML gem now and create empty files.

To install the gem, we will add it to the Gemfile and run `bundle install`. Add the following line to the Gemfile and run `bundle install`:

```
gem 'haml', '4.0.6'
```

This will install the HAML gem.

Let's now add code to each of the routes and methods to the model wherever required. We will start in the order in which we have defined the routes.

Showing a page for all the existing lists

The responsibility for this request is showing all the available lists. We have already written the code to call the model method (`List.all`). The method is already defined by the sequel ORM library that we are using and hence, we don't need to add anything to the model. We just have to load an HTML page and pass the `lists` variable to it:

```
12    get '/?' do
13      all_lists =  List.all
14        haml :lists, locals: {lists: all_lists}
15    end
```

What we have added here is a call to the `haml` method that is defined by the `haml` gem. We have passed two parameters to it, namely, `:lists` and `locals: {lists: lists}`.

The first argument is the name of the `haml` file. By default, the file is searched for in the `views` folder. So, we will create an empty file named `lists.haml` in the `views` folder. The filename and parameter should be the same.

The second parameter is called `locals`. Locals are used to pass values to the `haml` page. When we design `lists.haml`, we can access a variable named `lists` that will have the value of the `all_lists` variable.

Showing a page to create a new list

The responsibility of this request is just to show an HTML page where the user can enter data for a new list. So, we replace the comment with a `haml` call to the `new_list` page. Again, we have to create a new file named `new_list` in the `views` folder. Here is the code:

```
17    get '/new/?' do
18      haml :new_list
19    end
```

There is no need for any `locals` here.

Handling the saving of a new list

When the user submits the form to create a new list, the request will be handled here. The application has a variable named `params` that will have the form values. We can use this variable and create our list. We will design the form in such a way that it has a `name` field (the title of the list) and an array of items, each element having `name` and `description`. These values will be accessible in the `params` variable. The following is the code:

```
21    post '/new/?' do
22      user = User.first(name: session[:user_id])
23      List.new_list params[:title], params[:items], user
24      redirect request.referer
25    end
```

In line 22, we fetch the user record for the currently logged in user from the `User` class. The first method is already defined by sequel. The value of `user_id` is taken from the `session` variable. We will see how to use `session` later in this chapter.

In line 23, we call the `new_list` method of the `List` class and pass the values of `title` and `items`. We will need to define this method and create a new list.

In line 24, we redirect to the HTML page from which the request originally came.

The `new_list` method (in `models/list.rb`) will be:

```
10      def self.new_list name, items, user
11        list = List.create(name: name, created_at: Time.now)
12        items.each do |item|
13          Item.create(name: item[:name], description:
            item[:description], list: list, user: user,
              created_at: Time.now, updated_at: Time.now)
14        end
15        Permission.create(list: list, user: user,
            permission_level: 'read_write', created_at: Time.now,
              updated_at: Time.now)
16
17        return list
18      end
```

Let's go through this method line by line:

- Line 10: This defines a method named `new_list` that accepts three parameters, namely, `name`, `items`, and `user`.

- Line 11: This creates a list with `name` as the value of the `name` variable and `created_at` as the value of `Time.now`. The `create` adds a new record and this method is defined by `sequel`. `Time.now` returns the current time.

- Lines 12-14: This iterates over the `items` array and creates a new record for each `item`. It adds the `list` and `user` information to the `item`.

- Line 15: This creates a record in the `permissions` table with a `read_write` permission to the current user on the newly created list.

- Line 17: This returns the list.

Showing a page to edit a list

When a user tries to edit a list, we will first check whether the user has the correct permission to edit the list or not. If the user has the correct permissions, then we will show the edit page. Here is the code for it:

```
27    get '/edit/:id/?' do
28      list = List.first(id: params[:id])
29      can_edit = true
30
31      if list.nil?
32        can_edit = false
33      elsif list.shared_with == 'public'
34        user = User.first(id: session[:user_id])
```

```
35        permission = Permission.first(list: list, user: user)
36        if permission.nil? or permission.permission_level ==
          'read_only'
37          can_edit = false
38        end
39      end
40
41      if can_edit
42        haml :edit_list, locals: {list: list}
43      else
44        haml :error, locals: {error: 'Invalid permissions'}
45      end
46    end
```

This block checks whether the currently logged in user has correct permissions on the list or not and shows the edit or error page accordingly.

Let's go through the code line by line:

- Line 28: This gets the record for the list
- Line 29: This sets the value of the can_edit variable to true
- Lines 31-39: If the list id passed is incorrect, the value of the list variable will be nil and can_edit will be set to false

If the permission on the list is not public, we find the permission of the user on the list. If the user does not have any permission, the value of the permission variable will be nil as there will be no record in the database and hence, can_edit will be set to false.

If the permission exists but is read_only, then can_edit will be set to false.

Lines 41-45: This loads the edit_list haml if can_edit is true and error haml if can_edit is false.

Here, we have to create edit_list.haml and error.haml in the views folder.

Handling the updating of a list

We will pass the form data to the edit_list method of the list class. This method will update the list name, delete all the items that are marked for deletion (we will pass a delete value from the HTML), and add any new items. The following is the code:

```
48    post '/edit/?' do
49      user = User.first(id: session[:user_id])
```

```
50      List.edit_list params[:id], params[:name], params[:items],
        user
51      redirect request.referer
52    end
```

The `edit_list` method in the `List` class will be as follows:

```
20      def self.edit_list id, name, items, user
21        list = List.first(id: id)
22        list.name = name
23        list.updated_at = Time.now
24        list.save
25
26        items.each do |item|
27          if item[:deleted]
28            i = Item.first(item[:id]).destroy
29            next
30          end
31          i = Item.first(item[:id])
32          if i.nil?
33            Item.create(name: item[:name], description:
            item[:description], list: list, user: user,
                created_at: Time.now, updated_at: Time.now)
34          else
35            i.name = item[:name]
36            i.description = item[:description]
37            i.updated_at = Time.now
38            i.save
39          end
40        end
41      end
```

Let's go through this method line by line:

- Line 20: This defines a method named `edit_list` that accepts four parameters, namely, `id`, `name`, `items`, and `user`. The `id` is the ID of the list, `name` is the new name, `items` is the array of the items, and `user` is the currently logged in user.

- Lines 21-24: This fetches the list and updates the `name`.

- Lines 26-40: This iterates over the `items` array and, if there is a `deleted` key in the `item` object, it deletes the object and skips the rest of the loop. Otherwise, it searches for the item in the database and edits the `name`, `description`, and `updated_at` if the item is found or creates it.

Changing permissions on a list

The HTML page will submit the list ID, new permission, and permission level. The code will validate the user's current permission and update the database with the new permissions:

```
54    post '/permission/?' do
55      user = User.first(id: session[:user_id])
56      list = List.first(id: params[:id])
57      can_change_permission = true
58
59      if list.nil?
60        can_change_permission = false
61      elsif list.shared_with != 'public'
62        permission = Permission.first(list: list, user: user)
63        if permission.nil? or permission.permission_level ==
           'read_only'
64          can_change_permission = false
65        end
66      end
67
68      if can_change_permission
69        list.permission = params[:new_permissions]
70        list.save
71
72        current_permissions = Permission.first(list: list)
73        current_permissions.each do |perm|
74          perm.destroy
75        end
76
77        if params[:new_permissions] == 'private' or parms[:new_
           permissions] == 'shared'
78          user_perms.each do |perm|
79            u = User.first(perm[:user])
80            Permission.create(list: list, user: u, permission_
             level: perm[:level], created_at: Time.now,
             updated_at: Time.now)
81          end
82        end
83
84        redirect request.referer
85      else
86        haml :error, locals: {error: 'Invalid permissions'}
87      end
88    end
```

This block checks whether the currently logged in user can edit the permissions on the given list or not. If yes, it deletes all the old permissions and sets the new permissions. We will design our HTML form in such a way that it submits the list id and new permission (private, shared, or public) and an array of users with their permission levels (read_only or read_write) if the list is made shared. If the list is made private, the array of users will have the currently logged user and level as read_write.

Let's go through this code line by line:

- Line 55: This gets the record of the currently logged in user.
- Line 56: This gets the record of the list.
- Line 57: This sets the value of the can_change_permission variable to true.
- Lines 59-66: This checks whether the user has permissions to edit the list. If not, it changes the value of the can_change_permission variable to false.
- This is the same as we did in the edit_list route.
- Lines 68-87: If can_change_permission is true, it updates the list's permission value and deletes all the existing permissions. It also sets the permissions for all the users with the permission level as specified if the list is made private or shared. Otherwise, it shows the error page.

Showing a page for signup

This route will show an HTML for a new user to sign up. Here is the code:

```
90    get '/signup/?' do
91      if session[:user_id].nil?
92        haml :signup
93      else
94        haml :error, locals: {error: 'Please log out first'}
95      end
96    end
```

We will need to create signup.haml in the views folder.

Saving the new user data

This route creates a new user in the User table. The following is the code:

```
98     post '/signup/?' do
99       md5sum = Digest::Md5.hexdigest params[:password]
100      User.create(name: params[:name], password: md5sum)
101    end
```

Line 99 creates an MD5 hash of the password.

Showing a page for login

This route shows the login page:

```
103    get '/login/?' do
104      if session[:user_id].nil?
105        haml :login
106      else
107        haml :error, locals: {error: 'Please log out first'}
108      end
109    end
```

We will need to create login.haml in the views folder.

Handling user login

This route checks whether the user credentials are valid or not and redirects to the appropriate HTML page. We will need to add one more line to app.rb to enable sessions in the configure block. Here is the line:

```
10 enable :sessions
```

We will add the following code to the route:

```
113    post '/login/?' do
114      md5sum = Digest::Md5.hexdigest params[:password]
115      user = User.first(name: params[:name], password: md5sum)
116      if user.nil?
117        haml :error, locals: {error: 'Invalid login
           credentials'}
118      else
119        session[:user_id] = user.id
120        redirect '/'
121      end
122    end
```

Handling user logout

This route clears the session of the currently logged in user and shows the login page. The following is the code:

```
124    get '/logout/?' do
125      session[:user_id] = nil
126      redirect '/login'
127    end
```

This code sets the `user_id` key of the `session` variable to `nil` and shows the `login` page.

Before we go ahead and start designing the frontend for the application, we have to add a small piece of code to make sure that the user is logged in every time we receive a request. This will make sure that all the routes can be accessed only when we have a valid user.

It will be quite repetitive if we have to write the same code inside every route. To do this efficiently, we will use Sinatra's `before` block.

Understanding before and after blocks

There are times when we need to execute a piece of code before (or after) executing any route. To avoid writing such codes repetitively, we can use the `before` or `after` block as required. As the name suggests, the `before` block gets invoked before the route is executed and the `after` block gets invoked after the route is executed.

In our case, we need to check the validity of the user's session before executing the route. So, we will add the following code:

```
14    before do
15      if not request.path_info.split('/')[1] == 'login' and
         session[:user_id].nil?
16        redirect '/login'
17      end
18    end
```

This block will be invoked for every route. Note that the order in which the routes or the `before`/`after` blocks are written does not matter.

The new thing that we have used in this block is the `request` object in line 15. The `request` object holds the metadata for the request made to the server, such as the URL, port, user agent, referer, and so on.

We use `path_info` to find the path from which the request was made. This block redirects the user to the login page only if the `session[:user_id]` is `nil`, which means that the user is not logged in. We also check the path to avoid a redirect loop and so the `before` block will only redirect to the login page if the request is not on the login page.

The `request.path_info` will return something like `'/foo'`. We use the split method on this string to split the path based on the occurrence of `'/'`. This will return an array of strings. Hence, splitting `'/login'`, `'/login/'`, and `'/login/foo'` will return `["", "login"]`, `["", "login"]`, and `["", "login", "foo"]` respectively. We see that the the first element of this array is always `"login"`. Hence, `request.path_info.split('/')[1]` will be a foolproof way to check whether the request was indeed to the login page or not.

Summary

In this chapter, we discussed how to design routes and add methods to the model. We saw how `sessions` can be used to pass user information across requests and perform basic operations on lists, such as create, fetch, edit, delete, and so on. We also used the `before` block to easily check for valid user sessions. Additionally, using an ORM made the task a lot simpler than writing raw SQL queries. In the next chapter, we will see how to design HTML pages using HAML.

6
Designing the Frontend Layout

In the previous chapter, we made our application listen to requests from the user and process them. Our ToDo application's server-side part is done. Now, all that remains is designing the user interface to provide the user with an easy way to navigate through the system.

In this chapter, we will discuss the following topics:

- How to use the Twitter Bootstrap CSS framework and jQuery
- How to write `Haml` templates

Understanding Twitter Bootstrap and jQuery

Twitter Bootstrap (`http://getbootstrap.com/`) is an open source CSS framework that is being used widely by developers to design beautiful web-based applications quickly. It has very descriptive documentation and provides various components that can be used by us. Before we begin writing any code, we should go through the website (`http://getbootstrap.com/getting-started/`) and take a brief look at the resources that it has.

To use Bootstrap effectively, we need jQuery (`http://jquery.com/`) too. The jQuery is a JavaScript library that provides extensive functions and plugins to design web-based applications.

After we are done going through the websites of Bootstrap and jQuery, let's download the packages that they provide. We will download the minified versions of both these frameworks as we are not going to edit them. A minified version provides the exact same functionality but is smaller in size; it is just not easy to read. Furthermore, as we are not going to edit them anyway, readability is not an issue.

At the time of writing this, the available Bootstrap version is 3.3.2 and the jQuery version is 1.11.2. We will use these versions to write our application.

The Bootstrap 3.3.2 package contains three folders: `js`, `css`, and `fonts`. So we will create a folder named `public` in our application's root directory. We will create the same three subfolders in the `public` folder—`js`, `css`, and `fonts`—and then copy the contents one by one.

Next, we will copy `bootstrap.min.js` to the `public/js` folder, `bootstrap.min.css` and `bootstrap-theme.min.css` to the `public/css` folder, and all the contents of `fonts` to the `public/fonts` folder. We will also copy `jquery-1.11.2.min.js` to the `public/js` folder.

The final structure of the `public` folder would be as follows:

```
public/
├── css
│   ├── bootstrap.min.css
│   └── bootstrap-theme.min.css
├── fonts
│   ├── glyphicons-halflings-regular.eot
│   ├── glyphicons-halflings-regular.svg
│   ├── glyphicons-halflings-regular.ttf
│   ├── glyphicons-halflings-regular.woff
│   └── glyphicons-halflings-regular.woff2
└── js
    ├── bootstrap.min.js
    └── jquery-1.11.2.min.js
```

Now we can start writing the `haml` templates while using the Bootstrap and jQuery components.

Writing haml templates

The **HTML Abstraction Markup Language (HAML)** is a templating language that helps write clean and simple HTML templates. haml produces HTML when processed and also provides you with the scope to write inline Ruby statements.

Some basic things to keep in mind while writing haml templates are as follows:

Use % to define any HTML tag, such as `%table` for `<table>` or `%head` for `<head>`.

- Use two spaces of indentation to define child elements and autogenerate closing tags
- Use a hash to add HTML attributes, such as `%form{name: "some-form"}`
- Use . to add a class and # to add an ID instead of explicitly specifying them in the hash, such as `%form.form#signup` for `<form class="form" id="signup">` instead of `%form{class: "form", id: "signup"}`
- Instead of defining `<div>` using `%div.class#id`, use `.class#id` directly. The equivalent HTML would be `<div class="class" id="id>`

Sinatra has a unique way of dealing with haml. All the haml files will be stored in the `views/` folder. By default, this is the folder that Sinatra looks in whenever it has to load haml. It also understands a file named `layout.haml` as a special haml file. We use the layout file to design common components of different web pages, such as the header, footer, and so on.

So, let's start designing the UI by writing the layout file.

Writing layout.haml

All of our web pages will have a common header and use some additional css rules that are not defined in Bootstrap's framework. So, let's see how the code goes and understand it line by line:

```
!!! 5
%html
  %head
    %title ToDo
    %script{src: "/js/jquery-1.11.2.min.js"}
    %script{src: "/js/bootstrap.min.js"}
    %link{rel: "stylesheet", href: "/css/bootstrap.min.css"}
    %link{rel: "stylesheet", href: "/css/bootstrap-theme.min.css"}

    :css
      .has-below {
        padding-bottom: 20px;
      }

  %body
    .container-fluid
```

```
          .col-md-12
            .row
              %nav.navbar.navbar-inverse.navbar-fixed-
      top{role:'navigation'}
                  .navbar-inner
                    .container-fluid
                      .navbar-header
                        %button.navbar-toggle{data:{toggle:'collapse'}}
                          %span.icon-bar
                          %span.icon-bar
                          %span.icon-bar
                        %a.navbar-brand{href: url('/')}
                          %i.glyphicon.glyphicon-home
                          Home

              .has-below
              .has-below
              .has-below

          .row
            =yield
```

If we go through the points to keep in mind that were mentioned in the previous section, we can understand what the equivalent HTML code would look like except for a few lines. Let's go through the code line by line:

Line 1: !!!5 is how we define <!DOCTYPE HTML>. This is information to the browser about the HTML version that the web page is using. As all our web pages will be using version 5, we add this as the first line of our layout file.

Line 2: %html generates the <html> tag. Every other tag will be indented under it.

Lines 3-8: This defines the <head> block. Note the indentation done in lines 3-8. This makes sure that the <title>, <script>, and <link> tags are added within <head>. The <title> adds a title to the web page and <script> and <link> include the css and js files respectively.

Lines 10-13: We use :css to define internal css rules. The :css will generate a <style> tag and add the rules within it. We have written a style that says that an element with the has-below class will have padding-bottom of 20px.

We can see that lines 3-13 are indented under line 2. This makes sure that the title, css, and js are children to <head>.

Line 15: %body is indented at the same level as %head. This would generate </head> and <body>. So, whenever we indent a tag at the same level as a previous one, haml generates a corresponding closing tag too.

Lines 16-33: This is written as specified by Bootstrap's documentation. Lines 19-29 add navbar (http://getbootstrap.com/components/#navbar) to the top of the page and lines 31-33 are used to add some padding.

Lines 35-36: We see a new thing here, = yield. In haml, = is used to execute a ruby statement and print its output. The yield function is a ruby method that invokes a block pass. If we see how we have defined our routes, we would find lines such as haml :login or haml :signup and so on. In this case, :login or :signup are the blocks passed.

Hence, = yield will invoke the specific haml page passed and include the contents while rendering the HTML.

So, when we design other individual web pages, it will be clearer how yield functions.

We will now design the signup form.

Writing signup.haml

Before anyone can use this application, a user must be created. A signup page would have the form to create a user. The code would be as follows:

```
.col-md-4.col-md-offset-4
  .has-below
  .has-below
  .has-below
  .has-below
  .has-below
  .panel.panel-primary
    .panel-heading
      %h3.panel-title Signup
    .panel-body
      %form.form-horizontal{name: "signup", method: "post",
      action: url("/signup")}
        .form-group
          %label.control-label.col-md-3{for: "name"} Username
          .col-md-8
            %input.form-control{type: "text", name: "name"}
        .form-group
          %label.control-label.col-md-3{for: "password"} Password
          .col-md-8
```

```
      %input.form-control{type: "password", name: "password"}
    .form-group
      .col-md-2.col-md-offset-3
        %button.btn.btn-sm.btn-primary{type: "submit"}
          %i.glyphicon.glyphicon-ok
          Submit
```

The code has nothing new in it. It uses the Bootstrap panel (http://getbootstrap. com/components/#panels) and Bootstrap form (http://getbootstrap.com/ components/#panels). This code will generate the following HTML:

```
<!DOCTYPE html>
<html>
  <head>
    <title>ToDo</title>
    <script src='/js/jquery-1.11.2.min.js'></script>
    <script src='/js/bootstrap.min.js'></script>
    <link href='/css/bootstrap.min.css' rel='stylesheet'>
    <link href='/css/bootstrap-theme.min.css' rel='stylesheet'>
    <style>
      .has-below {
        padding-bottom: 20px;
      }
    </style>
  </head>
  <body>
    <div class='container-fluid'>
      <div class='col-md-12'>
        <div class='row'>
          <nav class='navbar navbar-inverse navbar-fixed-top'
          role='navigation'>
            <div class='navbar-inner'>
              <div class='container-fluid'>
                <div class='navbar-header'>
                  <button class='navbar-toggle'
                  data-toggle='collapse'>
                    <span class='icon-bar'></span>
                    <span class='icon-bar'></span>
                    <span class='icon-bar'></span>
                  </button>
                  <a class='navbar-brand'
                  href='http://localhost:9292/'>
                    <i class='glyphicon glyphicon-home'></i>
                    Home
                  </a>
```

```
              </div>
            </div>
          </div>
        </nav>
        <div class='has-below'></div>
        <div class='has-below'></div>
        <div class='has-below'></div>
      </div>
      <div class='row'>
        <div class='col-md-4 col-md-offset-4'>
          <div class='has-below'></div>
          <div class='has-below'></div>
          <div class='has-below'></div>
          <div class='has-below'></div>
          <div class='has-below'></div>
          <div class='panel panel-primary'>
            <div class='panel-heading'>
              <h3 class='panel-title'>Signup</h3>
            </div>
            <div class='panel-body'>
              <form action='http://localhost:9292/signup'
class='form-horizontal' method='post' name='signup'>
                <div class='form-group'>
                  <label class='control-label col-md-3'
for='name'>Username</label>
                  <div class='col-md-8'>
                    <input class='form-control' name='name'
type='text'>
                  </div>
                </div>
                <div class='form-group'>
                  <label class='control-label col-md-3'
for='password'>Password</label>
                  <div class='col-md-8'>
                    <input class='form-control' name='password'
type='password'>
                  </div>
                </div>
                <div class='form-group'>
                  <div class='col-md-2 col-md-offset-3'>
                    <button class='btn btn-sm btn-primary'
type='submit'>
                      <i class='glyphicon glyphicon-ok'></i>
                      Submit
                    </button>
```

```
                </div>
              </div>
            </form>
          </div>
        </div>
      </div>
    </div>
  </div>
  </body>
</html>
```

In this HTML, lines 1-40 and lines 77-81 are generated by the layout file and lines 41-76 are generated by the signup haml file. We now see how the `yield` method in the layout file has inserted the block generated by the signup haml to produce a single HTML page.

Summary

In this chapter, we saw how we can use HAML and get away with writing HTML. We also saw how to use Twitter Bootstrap and design beautiful web pages quickly.

In the next chapter, we will see how to write the other views and use more of Twitter Bootstrap and jQuery to make our application look beautiful and work seamlessly.

7
Handling User Data

In the previous chapter, we made the forms and designed them, and now we are able to see the form where a user can fill in data and use the application. A well-designed user interface is very important. Now we will make these forms functional and handle the data provided by the user.

In this chapter, you will learn the following topics:

- Creating forms
- Handling data in the backend

Creating forms

Here, you are going to learn how to work with forms. We know that to be able to create a list and its tasks, we need to give the user an interface where he will fill in the data, submit the form and the data will go to the server, then the server processes the data and creates a list of tasks for the user.

A quick overview of the HTML form tag

Forms are needed when we want to collect some data from the user. For example, during user login, we ask the user to fill in name and password. For name and password we used input element with text and password type. Like the text and password, there are various form elements available such as the text area fields, drop-down menus, radio buttons, checkboxes, and so on.

A form tag has as many attributes as any other HTML tag and we are not going to discuss each and every attribute here as it is out of the scope of our goal.

If you are interested, then you can check out some online guides such as w3schools (http://www.w3schools.com/html/html_forms.asp).

We are interested here in two main attributes of the form tag, which are `action` and `method`. Both of these attributes help us while we define the routing of our application. They help us in identifying HTTP methods (verbs) and the URL. We will explain `action` and `method` in more detail:

- **Action**: In this attribute, we specify the URL of the request. Whenever a form gets submitted, it sends data to the server and specific URL, this URL will be placed in the value of this attribute. For example, in the last chapter, when we were designing the signup form, we placed `/signup` as the value of the `action` attribute. In this way, that form will submit the request to the `/signup` URL.

- **Method**: In this attribute, we specify the HTTP request `type`, `method`, or `verb` (others may use the word of their convention). So basically, whenever we specify a request (URL) for the server, we must specify the request type so that the server can map it to the correct code/method (that is, if it is a GET request, POST request, PUT, or DELETE). As shown in the previous examples, we use one of these methods with URLs and the corresponding code for them.

```
# show create list page
get '/new/?' do
  haml :new_list
end

# show create list page
post '/new/?' do
  user = User.first(name: session[:user_id])
  List.new_list params[:title], params[:items], user
  redirect request.referer
end
```

Here, we can observe in the code that it is the combination of both pages required on the server side to determine the exact request and its corresponding processing.

Writing new_list.haml

Now we know the basics of the form tag with necessary attributes, and we also know that we want to give our users an option to create/add their list and items in the list. So, let's create the interface from where the user can add a new list and add multiple items to its list.

Let's recall what we want to achieve. When a user is creating a list, he should be able to give a `name` to the list and add multiple `items` to the list. An `item` will have a `name` and `description`.

Now, let's write the code and understand it line by line:

```
.col-md-8.col-md-offset-2
  .has-below
  .panel.panel-primary
    .panel-heading
      %h3.panel-title Create List
    .panel-body
      %form.form-horizontal{name: "list", method: "post", action:
url("/new")}
        .form-group
          %label.control-label.col-md-4{for: "name"} List Name
          .col-md-8
            %input.form-control{type: "text", name: "name"}
        %hr
        .form-group.item-group
          .col-md-4
            %input.form-control{type: "text", name: "items[][name]",
placeholder: "Item name"}
          .col-md-8
            %textarea.form-control{type: "text", name: "items[]
[description]", placeholder: "Item description"}
        #items_list.form-group
          %a{href: 'javascript:void(0)', id: 'add-item', class:
'col-md-3'} Add Item
        %hr
        .form-group
          .col-md-2.col-md-offset-3
            %button.btn.btn-sm.btn-primary{type: "submit"}
              %i.glyphicon.glyphicon-ok
              Create

  %script{type: "text/template", id: 'item_template'}
    .form-group.item-group
      .col-md-4
        %input.form-control{type: "text", name: "items[][name]",
placeholder: "Item name"}
      .col-md-8
        %textarea.form-control{type: "text", name: "items[]
[description]", placeholder: "Item description"}


  :javascript
    $(document).on('click', '#add-item', function(){
      var template_text = $('#item_template').html()
      $('#items_list').before(template_text);
});
```

Line 1-4: These are the Bootstrap-related classes (`http://getbootstrap.com/`) that will create divs (div tags) to make our page look clean.

Line 5: It will create a heading tag with a content Create List and Bootstrap-related class.

Line 7: Here is the first thing to note. It will create a form tag with `method: post` and `action: url(/new)`. When the user submits the form, the request will go to the `/new` URLs with the `post` method (as we discussed previously) with all the values in the form input elements that the user filled in. The form will be created with the `form-horizontal` class, which will use Bootstrap's design to make our form good and clean (as shown in the screenshot after this section).

Line 8: This is another Bootstrap set of classes that will be used to group related input elements so that they look related to the user.

Line 9: This creates a `label` tag with Bootstrap-related classes and content List Name. Label will be created with the `for` attribute that specifies which input element this label tag is created for.

Line 11: It will create an input element of the `text` type with the name as `name` where the user types in the name of the list that he is going to create.

Line 12: This simply draws a horizontal line, used to separate the `List` attributes from `Item` attributes.

Line 13: It will create another form-group of a group of related elements. It has another `item-group` class that we will use further. We are adding this class to mark and further identify the multiple items for a list, as we already know that a list will have multiple items.

Line 15: It will create an input element for the name attribute of an item; it will be an input element of the `text` type. A new or special thing is the `name` attribute here that has the `items[][name]` value. If you are not familiar with this type of notation, then let me tell you that it is to denote that we are going to have arrays of items. The `[]` denotes the array for its left-hand side attribute, which is `items` in our case. With the help of this notation, we will get the array of items on the server side when the user fills in and submits this form, and then we will process the array and create items for the list. This will create an `items` array with hash attributes and the current one is for name. We will look into the exact outcome later in this chapter

Line 17: As explained previously, this will create the `items` array for the `description` attribute.

Basically, with lines 15 and 17, we will get something as follows:

```
"items" => [{"name"=> "…", "description"=> "…"}, ….]
```

Line 18: This will create a special form group with the `items_list` ID, which is special because we will add some functionality around it later in our code.

Line 19: It will create a link with the content Add Item and the `add-item` ID with `href = "javascript:void(0)`, which means that we are creating this link for something but not directing it to any other page. The purpose of this link as its content is to tell `add item`. We have written some JavaScript magic around this link, which is whenever the user clicks on this link, we will add a new pair of fields/attributes for the item.

Line 21-25: It will create a separate section in which we are placing the `submit` button. Whenever the user clicks on this button, then the form will be submitted to the server.

Line 27-32: This is interesting. We are just creating a script tag with the `text/template` type and the `item_template` ID. You must be wondering what this `text/template` type is. This is just a type that I chose to set, and as the browser doesn't know about this type, it'll not process it and do nothing with it. Now then, why did we create it? The answer is that we created this for our own usage and we really wanted that the browser should not process it. Let me tell you what this solves for us. In our application, the user is free to add as many items as he wants to a list and for this, we needed to have a blank template kind of thing of items so that we can provide it to the user whenever he wants to add an item to the list. So, we created this blank template of items' attributes and kept it on the page (frontend) so that we can add new item fields to the form whenever we want.

Line 35: We want to write some inline JavaScript in the page; how can we do this with HAML? The `:javascript` filter is the answer. Now under this filter, we can write inline JavaScript code for the page, just like we write inline JavaScript in the `script` tag (`<script type='text/javascript'>…</script>`).

Line 36: Here, we are attaching the `click` event of the element with the `add-item` ID, which is the `Add Item` link in our case, with an anonymous function using jQuery's `on` method (check the jQuery documentation for further reference). Now whenever the user clicks on the `Add Item` link, then the code written in the anonymous function will be executed.

Line 37: Here, we can find our template of item attributes with it's ID, `item_template`, using jQuery and storing its HTML content in a local variable.

Line 38: Here, we can find the special element with the `items_list` ID (we are calling this item special because we are using it to mark the end of all the items' elements). As we are using it as the end of all the items list, we know that whenever we have to add a new field set for the item, we can add the new item just before the end mark; this is what we are doing here in our code using jQuery. We have our item template HTML element ready in a variable, we know where to place the template HTML, just before the end mark, so we find our end mark element with the `items_list` ID and place the template HTML just before this element using jQuery's `before` function.

Now our form is ready. When we place the `http://localhost:4567/new` URL in the browser, then our page will look as follows:

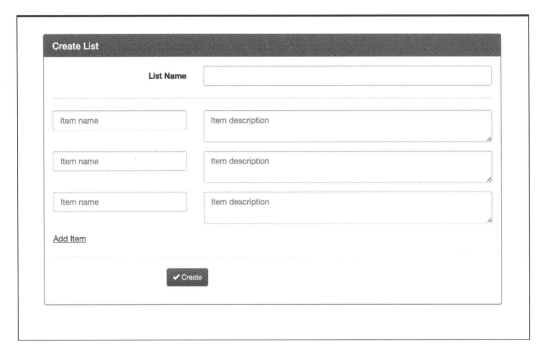

Our form is ready to be used by users, so when the user fills the data in it and clicks on **Create** button, then we have to handle the form data on the backend (server side). In the next section, let's see how we can do this.

Handling data in the backend

When the user clicks on the **Create** button, the browser looks at the method and action attributes and, in turn, sends the request to the server with the given URL by the specified method and data filled in by the user. Now, to handle this request, we have to write code on the server side to accept and process the request. We will write the code in our `app.rb` file or if we have a different routes file, `routes.rb`, then we will place the following code there:

```
# create list
post '/new/?' do
  user = User.first(id: session[:user_id])
  list = List.new_list params[:name], params[:items], user
  redirect "/lists/#{list.id}"
end
```

 Note: Whatever data the user filled in the form, will be accessible by the `params` method.

Let's take a quick walkthrough of this code:

Line 2: We are using a POST method to handle this request and it should already be specified in our form method attribute. Likewise, we also placed the URL in the action of our form, which matches the preceding specified string. Now, the method accepts the block of code and will execute it whenever a request comes.

Line 3: Here, we are fetching the current user with it's ID stored in the session state. We need to find the current user so that we can map the association while creating the list and add this user as the creator/owner of the list.

Line 4: We know that whatever data the user filled in the form will be available to us via `params`, so to process this data, we send the user data to the model and there we will corresponding list and items record. Here, we are just following the fact model convention and skinny controller convention, doing all the heavy processing on the model layer.

Line 5: After the creation of a list, we are just redirecting the user to the show page of the list.

Now let's look at the model layer processing and see how we are processing data here. Here is the code of the List model:

```
class List < Sequel::Model
  ...
  one_to_many :items
```

```
    ...

    def self.new_list(name, items, user)
      list = List.create name: name, created_at: Time.now
      items.each do |item|
        Item.create(name: item[:name], description: item[:description],
  list: list,
                    user: user, created_at: Time.now, updated_at: Time.
  now)
      end
      ...
      list
    end
  end
```

The code is pretty straightforward here: we defined the method that we are calling from our request handler code in which `name`, `items`, and `user` are passed as arguments.

Line: 7: This creates a list record with the name provided by the user with `created_at` added as the current time.

Line 8: This iterates the list (Array) of items added by the user. It will be something as follows:

```
"items"=>[{"name"=>"...", "description"=>"...."}, {"name"=>"...",
"description"=>"...."}, ...]
```

Line 9: Now we know that the item will have data such as `{"name"=>"...", "description"=>"...."}` with the name and description of the item. We have the user object for which we are creating items (item owner). We have the user object for which we are creating items (item owner). We have the list object in which these items are going to be added. That is all needed to create items in a list of a user so we creating it here.

Line 13: We are returning the newly created list so that our request handler or caller of the method can use the newly created list.

Validations

As of now, we are blindly trusting the user on the data end and expecting that the user will always fill in the correct data, but life is never that easy! Sometimes, deliberately or by mistake, attempts to save records with invalid data can happen (and it happens a lot in the real world). So how can we protect or stop these attempts? The answer is by adding validations.

We can add two types of validations to the application:

- Frontend validations
- Backend validations

Frontend Validations

This is also known as client-side validations because everything related to this type of validation exists on the client side only (for example, the browser). There are two common ways of doing client-side validations: client-side form validations with HTML5 and client-side validations with JavaScript. We will see a very quick overview of these:

Client-side validation with JavaScript: You can write JavaScript code to validate the data filled in by the user and stop the data being sent to the server. You can achieve this by attaching your JavaScript functions in various JavaScript events, for instance, you can write a function that checks whether the input has some value or not and if some fields are empty, then you can halt the event and show the user the error message.

HTML5 form validation: This is one of the great features introduced by HTML5. For general validations such as required fields, matching a pattern, or validating numbers, e-mails, or URLs, we have to write JavaScript code and test it. HTML5 introduces new HTML attributes to achieve this in a very simple way. You just need to add a `type`, `pattern`, or `require` attribute to the `<input ..>` tag and you are ready to go. As in the `type` attribute, you can specify the type of the field such as the e-mail, number, or URL, and HTML handles the rest on its own—stopping the request being sent to the server and showing the error message on the field. HTML5 validation does this for you out of the box.

Backend Validations

We can do the validations that we discussed on the backend as well. The way of doing this varies from framework to framework. Now let's see how we can do this with Sinatra. We are validating data here and for data manipulation, we have created models. This means that model is the place where we write code to validate our data and prevent the creation/updating of data with invalid values. For example, we want the `name` field of the `List` model to be mandatory, so it will have a value. We can do this by adding the following code:

```
class List < Sequel::Model
  ...
  def validate
```

```
      super
      errors.add(:name, 'cannot be blank') if !name || name.empty?
      errors.add(:name, 'already taken') if name && new? &&
   List[:name=>name]
      errors.add(:name, 'not a valid name') unless name =~ /\A[A-Za-z]/
    end
  end
```

The way this works is whenever we try to create or update a record, `Sequel::Model` tries to validate the record by calling the `validate` method, and in this method, we can specify our own validations that we want enforced. We can also check the validation of an object by calling `valid?` on it.

Instead of writing our own validation code, we can also use the `validation_helpers` plugin of Sequel. All we need to do is add a line above the model as follows:

```
Sequel::Model.plugin :validation_helpers
class List < Sequel::Model
....
end
```

Then, we can use Sequel's `validation_helpers` methods as follows:

```
Sequel::Model.plugin :validation_helpers
class List < Sequel::Model
  ...
  def validate
    super
    validates_presence [:name, :created_at]
    validates_unique :name
    validates_format /\A[A-Za-z]/, :name, message: 'is not a valid
name'
  end
end
```

If frontend validations are so cool, then why do we want to add validation to the backend? Sometimes, the user can disable the JavaScript in the browser or use a browser that doesn't support HTML5 and we really cannot do anything about this. So, for this reason, we should add validations to the backend as well. Adding validations to the data layer (model) is strongly recommended to ensure that we are not allowing inconsistent data into the system from any source. Both frontend and backend validations are very important and should exist in the system.

Summary

In this chapter, you learned how to create a form and its necessary attributes and how it works. We saw the importance and usage of the method and action attributes of a form. We created a page to add a new list and multiple items in that list with a html form. You also learned how to add items to the form through JavaScript dynamically using a simple dummy template. We saw how we can handle user form data on the backend. You also learned about implementing validations and the types of validations.

In the next chapter, you will learn how to connect and communicate with the database in Sinatra.

8
Connecting to a Database

In the previous chapter, we created a user interface for users to add their lists and items to the list through an HTML form. You learned about the basics of the form and its attributes, how to handle the data submitted by a user on the server side, and how to prevent the user from entering wrong data in the application through validations. Now that valid data has reached the server side, let's persist the data for the users so that we can show it back to the user whenever the user wants. To achieve this, we need to store it to the database, which you are going to learn step by step in this chapter.

In this chapter, we will discuss the following topics:

- How to connect and communicate with a database
- How to use an ORM

Connecting to a database

As we know, our application has to store user data, and for this purpose, we chose MySQL, currently one of the more popular SQL databases. Now you will learn how our Ruby classes communicate with MySQL. The first thing that we have to do is update our `Gemfile` and add the following lines:

```
...
gem 'sequel', '4.25.0'
gem 'mysql', '2.9.1' #For MySQL
...
```

As you have already learned, some basics about the `sequel` gem are that it provides the ORM layer to our application, which we will cover later in this chapter. For now, it is enough to remember that we are using it for our models.

The next gem used is `mysql`, which is a ruby interface for MySQL. This gem will be used by Sequel to communicate with the MySQL database. Sequel can work with a number of databases such as MySQL, PostgreSQL, SQLite and others. We just need to specify the corresponding connector or adapter to it as an initial configuration with the corresponding library or gem.

Now, the question is how to specify the corresponding adapter and how this configuration is done? So the answer is that there are a lot of ways of doing this, different people do it differently, so we are choosing a very clean and popular way of doing things by creating a configuration file, `database.yml`. YAML (`http://yaml. org`) is a data serialization human friendly language and used very commonly in ruby development for configuration files. Let's look at this file and understand it step by step:

```
development:
    adapter: 'mysql'
    host: 'localhost'
    database: 'todo_development'
    user: 'root'
    password: 'password'
```

A similar approach is used by many frameworks and libraries such as ActiveRecord and Ruby on Rails, which use the `database.yml` file for database configuration.

Let's compile it step by step:

Line 1: We are scoping the database-related information here for different environments, for instance, we specified information for the development environment in the code. Everything under `development` is scoped for the development environment; similarly, we can specify database information for `test`, `staging`, `production`, or any custom environment for the application.

Line 2: Here, we are specifying the adapter of the database. With the help of this, Sequel will be able to figure out which database to connect with; in our case, it is MySQL.

Line 3: Here, we are specifying the hostname of the database server.

Line 4: Here, we are specifying the name of the database.

Line 5: Here, we are specifying the name of the database user that will be used in creating a connection with the database. The username here is your MySQL user, which you have created while setting up the MySQL server.

Line 6: Here, we are specifying the password of the database user, which will be used in creating a connection with the database.

Now that our configuration file is in place with all the necessary parameters, let's use these parameters and build a connection to the database. For this, you need to add the following code in `app.rb`:

```
class Todo < Sinatra::Base
  set :environment, ENV['RACK_ENV']

  configure do
    env = ENV['RACK_ENV']
    DB = Sequel.connect(YAML.load(File.open('database.yml'))[env])
    ...
  end
  ....
end
```

You have already learned about `app.rb` earlier in this book and we know that it is the main file or starting point of our application. Let's see step by step what we are doing in the file this time:

Line 2: The `set :environment` sets the current environment of the application, which should be `development` for the local machine and production for the production or live application. Similarly, we can have test, staging, and other environments. We can specify the current environment in the `config.ru` file (we will see this later) or we can specify it while starting up the server as follows:

```
RACK_ENV=staging rackup
```

Line 4: In the `configure` block, application-level variables and settings are specified, which are available within the request context. The block also accepts the environment name as an argument. Then, it will execute the code only for that specific environment; when we do not specify any environment, then the code in the block will be executed for every environment.

Line 5: Here, we are capturing the current environment name in a local variable to use it later in the code. It will be `development` on the local machine.

Line 6: This is the line to focus on. First, we are opening the `database.yml` file using the `File.open` method, which will return the file object that we are using `YAML::load` to load the `.yml` file content as a nested key-value pair or `Hash`. Then, from this configuration hash, we are selecting the configuration values for the current environment that is stored in the `env` variable. Basically, we fetched the database configuration options for the current environment and we are passing these options to Sequel who will use them to create the connection with the database; we are passing these values through the `Sequel.connect` method.

Now, let's look at the config.ru file where we are specifying the default environment value that will be used by it when we run our application:

```
require 'sinatra'
require 'bundler/setup'
Bundler.require

ENV["RACK_ENV"] = "development"
require File.join(File.dirname(__FILE__), 'app.rb')
Todo.start!
```

Line 5: Here, we are specifying the current environment that we will change for the production and staging either here or while running the server through the `rackup` command mentioned previously.

The rest of the commands have already been explained in *Chapter 3, Hello World*.

An interactive console

Now, we are connected to our database (MySQL), our models are mapped to their corresponding MySQL tables, and we can verify this from an interactive console. An interactive console is a very useful thing that lets you interact with your application from a terminal such as Bash (for Unix) or a command prompt (for Windows). It is awesome and I use it almost everyday. I use it for the querying and troubleshooting problems. Sinatra or Sequel has no out-of-the-box interactive console like this, but there is a very easy way of doing this by just typing the following command in your terminal:

```
RACK_ENV=development irb -r ./app.rb
```

We are not doing anything special here; we are just specifying the environment in the beginning with `RACK_ENV=development` and starting **interactive ruby session (irb)** with the `-r` option, which means open `irb` with the given file.

Now you have an irb session open with your application loaded; you can try to interact with the database through your models as follows:

```
2.2.1 :001 > User.count
 => 4
2.2.1 :002 > List.last
 => #<List @values={:id=>3, :name=>"My First List", :shared_
with=>"private", :created_at=>2015-08-30 14:16:57 +0530}>
```

Now I can say that we have successfully made the connection to the database from our application.

How to use an ORM

As we know, we have covered the basics of ORM and its benefits in an earlier chapter, and decided to use Sequel as our ORM. Now, we will see how to use Sequel step by step and explore what it provides so that we know what we can achieve with this, because knowing your tools is mandatory in order to use them properly.

We have added the `sequel` gem to our `Gemfile` and now the first thing that we need to do is require it in `app.rb` so that our application can use it:

```
require 'sinatra'
require 'sequel'
...
```

We have to define and run migrations to add or modify the database using Sequel, which you already learned in the previous chapters. Then, we have to define models corresponding to the tables that we want to include in our application, which we have already covered in detail, so here is the syntax. The `Model` class is a simple ruby class that is a subclass of `Sequel::Model`:

```
class User < Sequel::Model
...
end
```

Now we can create models like this and our application is ready, but wait—is this all that Sequel gives us? Is this all that is needed to create a production-ready application? My answer would be no—this is just a bare minimum setup to create the model or use Sequel. Sequel provides us with a lot more functionality than this, which we are going to explore now.

The Sequel model

Whenever a model is created, it fetches the schema information of the table from the database through the information provided to create a connection with the database and builds setter and getter methods of all the columns available in the table of the model. This enables us to get and set values to the attributes of the class as follows:

```
user = User.first
user.name               # => "Manoj"   // getter
user.name = 'Manish'   # => "Manish"  // setter
```

The Sequel model assumes the table name as a pluralized and underscored version of the name of the model. For instance, for the `User` model, the name should be assumed `users` by default. We can also get this information from the model itself. Let's fire up your interactive console and run the following command:

```
2.2.1 :001 > User.table_name
 => :users
```

We can also specify a custom table name for the model while creating the `model` class:

```
class User < Sequel::Model(:admin_users)
...
end
```

Some useful model class methods

In this section, we will look at some of the useful class-level methods that Sequel provides to our models.

db_schema

This method returns the schema information of the model from the database. It returns a hash where the keys are column names and values are hashes of information related to the column:

```
User.db_schema # =>

{:id=>
  {:primary_key=>true,
   :auto_increment=>true,
   :allow_null=>false,
   :default=>nil,
   :db_type=>"int(11)",
   :type=>:integer,
   :ruby_default=>nil},
 :name=>
  {:primary_key=>false,
   :allow_null=>false,
   :default=>nil,
   :db_type=>"varchar(255)",
   :type=>:string,
```

```
    :ruby_default=>nil,
    :max_length=>255}
  ...
}
```

columns

This method returns the column names' list of the model:

```
User.columns # => [:id, :name, :password, :created_at]
```

create

This method is used when we want to create a persistent object; in other words, when we want to insert a row in the table. We can pass the attributes hash to this method or a ruby block and assign values to attributes in it as follows:

```
User.create(name: 'Tom', password: 1234)

User.create do |u|
  u.name = 'Rob'
  u.password = '12345'
end
```

find_or_create

As the name suggests, this method finds and returns the object (if it exists) or creates a new one and returns it. Just like `create`, it also accepts a block and hash that it uses as a condition to find the record, and if the record does not exist, then it creates the object using the hash, but it uses a block only when it is going to create a new object. This method is very useful in production applications and I use it quite a bit in my code.

```
User.find_or_create(name: 'Tom', password: 1234)

User.find_or_create do |u|
  u.name = 'Rob'
  u.password = '12345'
end
```

def_column_alias

This method defines an alias to the given column name. It is helpful in situations where you have an attribute/column and you want to use it with a different name in different places. For example, you want to use the name attribute as username; you can do it as follows:

```
class User < Sequel::Model
  def_column_alias :username, :name
  ...
end

user.name        # => "Tom"
user.username    # => "Tom"
user.username = "Boby"
    user.name        # => "Boby"
```

first, first!, and last

These methods are used to fetch records of the model. The first is used to fetch the first record for the model if a record exists in the table; when the table has no records, this method will return nil.

Similarly, last is used to fetch the last object/record for the model if the record exists in the table; otherwise, it will also return nil.

The first! method will return the first element if it exists in the table; otherwise, it will raise an exception, Sequel::NoMatchingRow.

with_pk and with_pk!

The with_pk method is used to fetch the record for the given primary_key of the model if the record is found in the table for the primary key; otherwise, it will return nil:

```
User.with_pk(20)    # => <User @values={:id=>2, :name=>"Manoj",...
User.with_pk(900)   # => nil (for a user table without an id of 900)
```

The with_pk! method works just like with_pk; when the record exists for the primary key; otherwise, instead of returning nil, it throws a Sequel::NoMatchingRow exception.

finder

This method is used to create dynamic finders for your model. Let's say that we want to create a method such as `first_by_attr_name`. With the help of this method, we can efficiently do this. Let's take a look at the following code:

```
class User < Sequel::Model

  finder :by_id, type: :first
  finder :by_name, type: :first
  finder :by_name, type: :all

  def self.by_name(name)
    where(name: name)
  end

  def self.by_id(id)
    where(id: id)
  end
  ...
end
```

With the preceding code, our user model will now have the following methods available:

```
User.first_by_id(24)
User.first_by_name('Manoj')
User.all_by_name('Tom')
```

no_primary_key

This method is used in a very special scenario, where the model does not have a primary key. Although it is not recommended, in some edge cases, if the table of your model does not have a primary key constraint, you must notify Sequel about it. You can do this through this method:

```
class User < Sequel::Model
  no_primary_key
end
```

set_primary_key

This is used to set primary_key of the model. As we know, a primary key can be a regular key (with a single column) or it can be a composite key with multiple columns. We are going to see both of these types in the following example. If your model doesn't have primary_key, then you pass nil as an argument to this method to notify Sequel about it or you can use the no_primary_key method that we have just seen:

```
class User < Sequel::Model
  set_primary_key :id
  ...
end

class Permission < Sequel::Model
  set_primary_key [:user_id, :list_id]
  ...
end
```

restrict_primary_key and unrestrict_primary_key

The restrict_primary_key is used when you want to enable mass assignment on primary_key along with other attributes.

The unrestrict_primary_key is used when you do not want to enable mass assignment on primary_key.

set_allowed_columns

This method is used to set mass assignment on a given list of attributes. The attributes that are not present in the list will not be allowed in the mass assignment for the creation/update of an object and will raise an exception:

```
class User < Sequel::Model
  set_allowed_columns :name
end

User.set(name: 'Tom')      # Work fine
User.set(name: 'Tom', password: '1234') # Raise an exception
```

subset

The subset set allows us to specify commonly used queries that can be referenced as method calls on the models. With subset, we can use every query method. All subset methods will return a filtered dataset that will allow further methods (such as other subsets) to be called on it, which is called method chaining. Let's define subset in the User model:

```
class User < Sequel::Model
  subset :starts_with_m, Sequel.like(:name, 'm%')
  subset :early, ->{id < 100}
  ...
end
```

Now we can chain the subsets as follows:

```
User.starts_with_m.early
```

We will get all the users whose name starts with m and who were created early in our database, with an ID less than 100.

Useful model instance methods

Now we are going to see some useful methods of a model object or instance.

values or to_hash

We can use this method when we want our model object's attribute and their values to be hash. They will return the same result.

```
User.values  # => {:id=>1, :name=>"manoj", :password=>"".... }
User.to_hash # => {:id=>1, :name=>"manoj", :password=>"".... }
```

errors and valid?

You learned about the valid? method in the last chapter during validations. Now, if our object is not passing the validations defined, then errors is the method that will return the validation errors hash associated with the object:

```
list.valid? # => false
list.errors
#=> {:name=>["is not present"], :created_at=>["is not present"]}
```

exists?

This method can be used to verify that the object exists in the database or not; it will return `true` if it exists; otherwise, it will return `false`. In the case of a new object or deleted object, it will return `false`:

```
User.new.exists? # => false
```

changed_columns

This method returns all the columns that have changed their original values or values fetched from the database. This concept is also known as dirty tracking or dirty object tracking.

```
user.changed_columns # => []
user.name = 'Boby'
user.changed_columns # => [:name]
```

Once you save the object (in other words, sync with the database), then the `changed_columns` list resets to an empty array.

refresh or reload

This method is used to fetch the attributes' values of the object from the database; this can be used to ensure that we have the latest values of the attributes before updating it. It will return self as the response.

modified?

This method is used to check whether the object has been modified since it was last saved or not. In case it has been modified, it will return `true` and return `false` for a not unmodified object. New values of the attributes are always treated as modified values.

```
user.modified? # => false
user.name = 'John'
user.modified? # => true
```

new?

This method determines whether the current object is a new object or not, and returns `true` for a new object and `false` for an old one. The object is treated as old if it is a persisted object (that is, it exists in the database).

modified!

This method is used when we want to explicitly modify/update the object even if no attribute changes. This can be very useful in expiring cache fragments when we use the object's update timestamp. It will also run the callbacks or hooks.

save

This method is often used with model objects; it simply saves the object running all the validations and hooks. If all goes well, it returns `true` when it successfully saves the object; otherwise, it raises an exception when validation fails and returns `nil` when the hook halts the execution. If the object is new, it creates the object; otherwise, it updates the object.

delete

This method is used to delete the object; it does not run the callbacks or hooks:

```
user.delete
```

destroy

Just like `delete`, this method is also used to delete the object, but here, all callbacks or hooks will be executed and the object will be deleted only if all hooks run successfully and `before_destroy` does not return `false`, if it does, then it will not delete the object:

```
user.destroy
```

set

This method is used to set the attribute hashes that are allowed for mass assignment (through `allowed_columns`). It will raise an exception when an attribute in the passed hash is not allowed as part of mass assignment.

```
user.set( name: 'Rony')
```

set_all

This method is used to set the attributes hash irrespective of the mass assignment; it simply ignores the `allowed_columns` attributes list.

update

This method is similar to set but set just changes the values of the object in the memory and does not update it to the database until we call the save method on the object. Instead, update directly updates the changes to the database; we do not need to call save explicitly on the object.

update_all

This method is similar to set_all and like update, it updates the attributes of the object to the database and does not consider the allowed_columns list of attributes.

Hooks or callbacks

We can execute custom methods, logic, or code at different stages of the life cycle of the Sequel model object such as creating, updating, or deleting an object by defining hook or callback methods.

The before_validation and after_validation hook methods are triggered when validation of the object is checked; it happens when we use the valid? method or at the time of creating and updating the object.

The before_create and after_create hook methods are triggered when record creation happens.

The before_save and after_save hook methods are triggered when record creating and updating happens.

The before_update and after_update hook methods are triggered when a record is updated.

The before_destroy and after_destroy hook methods are triggered when the record deletion happens.

Here is an example of how we can define hooks:

```
class User < Sequel::Model
  ...
  def before_save
    super
    self.name = name.capitalize
  end
  ...
end
```

This is a very simple example of a hook where we are capitalizing the name of the user before saving it to the database using the `capitalize` method.

Associations

We know that whenever we create an application that needs a database, generally it requires many tables to store the data and relationships between these tables. On the database level, these are visualized using various tools such as an **Entity-Relationship Diagram (ERD)**. On the application level, these tables are now models that represent a business object, so to define the relationship between these business objects, we create an association using Sequel methods. These methods should be defined in the models. Here is an example to explain the possible types of association methods:

```
class User < Sequel::Model
  ....
  many_to_one :company
  one_to_many :addresses
  one_to_one :profile
  many_to_many :shopping_places
  one_through_one :first_shopping_place, class: :ShoppingPlace, order:
:place_name, right_key: :shopping_place_id
  ....
end
```

We have already covered the basics of associations in *Chapter 4, Modeling the Backend* so let's discuss some advanced things related to it.

Eager loading

This is a very useful concept with which we can improve the performance of the application drastically. You can eager load the associated objects and save the number of SQL queries to the database from the application, which is one of the most time-consuming part for any application. The concept is introduced as the solution to the N + 1 queries problem by fetching associated (or related) objects from the database at the same time that we are fetching our primary objects.

Associations can be eagerly loaded through the `:eager` association option that, instead of using a separate query to get the associated objects for each current object, loads all the associated objects in one query:

```
class List < Sequel::Model
  one_to_many :items, eager: [:user]
  ....
```

```
end

class Item < Sequel::Model
  many_to_one :user
  ....
end
```

We can also eager load the associations when we are fetching the records:

```
List.eager(:items).first
```

We can also eager load the associations with finders as follows:

```
User.early.eager(:permissions).all
```

We can do cascading of eager loading of the associations:

```
User.eager(:permissions =>:list).all
```

We can also pass Modeling the Backend to `Modeling the Backend` and specify conditions:

```
List.eager(items: proc{|e| e.where(Sequel.like(:description,
'%important%'))}).all
```

Joins with associations

Joins are one of the most powerful features of SQL. Like eager loading, we can use joins with associations to fetch results. Sequel provides you with a special method for this named `association_join`. This method can be used to add a join to the model's resulting dataset based on the association.

Here is its simple version:

```
Item.association_join(:user)
```

This will create a SQL query as follows:

```
# SELECT * FROM items
# INNER JOIN users AS user ON (user.id = item.user_id)
```

A join comes with other, similar methods corresponding to join types as follows:

```
List.association_left_join(:permissions)
```

Just like eager loading methods, we can use nested associations with join methods as well:

```
Item.association_join(:user, :list=>:permissions).all
```

Summary

In this chapter, you learned how to connect to a database (MySQL) with the necessary parameters and use the `mysql` gem with `sequel`. You also learned how to open and use the interactive console (irb) with Sinatra and Sequel. We covered the details of Sequel models with various useful class-level and instance-level methods. Next, we covered the available hooks and callbacks. Finally, we discussed associations with eager loading and joins in order to scale and optimize the application.

In the next chapter, you will learn how session works and implement authentication and authorization.

9
Authentication and Authorization

In the previous chapter, you learned how to connect a Sinatra application with the MySQL database, what gems are needed, and the configuration options. You learned about the interactive console (irb) and saw how we can use it to interact with Sequel models and methods. We then covered various methods that Sequel provides for the model, both class- and instance-level. We also discussed associations and related optimizations. Now that you have learned about models, let's use them to create user-specific data by remembering the user across the pages and requests.

In this chapter, we will cover the following topics:

- Using sessions
- Handling authentication using sessions

Using sessions in Sinatra

We know that HTTP is a stateless protocol and every request is like a new request to the server. A request has no idea about the previous request and whether there is a state maintained across the requests. However, today every application has to maintain state and give the user a personalized experience by remembering his preferences, choices, and other data such as authentication, but how can we do this with stateless protocol? The answer is sessions; sessions make it stateful. We are going find out what and how in this section.

What are sessions?

A session is a server-side storage of information for a user, which stores and updates the information for a user when required. In simple terms, a session is a Ruby hash for every user on the server in which we can store data as a key-value pair specific to that user. Generally, whenever a request is made and session is enabled, a session is created for the client user with `session_id`. Now, whenever we add or modify anything in the session data, we can access the session hash by this session_id.

How does it work?

Whenever the user opens a browser request, our application then creates a session and session_id is assigned to it. Then, we add the information to it for the user that we will need in future requests from the user. So the session hash is manipulated and session_id is sent in a cookie to that browser so that whenever the next request comes, it has session_id from the client. With session_id, we can fetch the user's session hash and get all the information about them that we stored previously.

In this way, we can remember the user and make our web application stateful with sessions.

Using the session variable

As we discussed earlier, session is just a hash build for an individual user and we can set any value, such as the following ruby hash for example:

```
session[:foo] = "bar"
```

In requests, we get this value using the same key:

```
session[:foo]
# => "bar"
```

It will be persisted across the requests for the user.

Enabling a session

Let me ask you a question: have you tried it in your code? If yes, then you must be scratching your head and asking yourself why this is not working. Why are my values not persisted across the requests? Have I done something wrong? The answer to all of your questions is that you are doing it all right but you just need to enable it.

Sinatra does not enable sessions for you by default; you have to enable it explicitly. The reason for this is that Sinatra is a very lightweight framework that is used for a variety of purposes. For example, you can build a completely static application or build an application as a web service (only for api). Sinatra doesn't know the exact use case of your application so session is not enabled by default, but you can enable session with just one line of code! Then you are ready with a session-enabled application. Let's see how we can enable a session for your `app.rb`:

```
require 'sinatra'
require 'sequel'

class Todo < Sinatra::Base
  set :environment, ENV['RACK_ENV']
  ....
  enable :sessions
  ....
end
```

The code is explained as follows:

Line 7: This is the setting that is responsible for enabling a session in your Sinatra application.

Now that you have enabled sessions, give your code another try. You will see that it works now and data is persisting across the requests.

Advanced options

This is the simplest setup to enable sessions. If you want to change other aspects of your session, then you can use `Rack::Session::Cookie` with options such as `domain`, `expire`, `secret`, and others:

```
require 'sinatra'
require 'sequel'

class Todo < Sinatra::Base
  set :environment, ENV['RACK_ENV']
  ....
  use Rack::Session::Cookie, :key => 'rack.session',
                             :domain => 'myawesomeapp.com',
                             :path => '/',
                             :expire_after => 2592000,
                             :secret => 'random_text',
                             :old_secret => 'another_random_text'

  ....
end
```

Methods of the session object

The Sinatra session also comes with some methods that we can use to provide additional capabilities. Here is a list of a few commonly used methods of session:

- **id**: Every session will have an ID as its identifier; it will be different (that is, unique) for every session object created:

```
session.id # =>
"2ce00a5a97e51374083ab15a623f6826d755fa55b9912f2ef703df72b5142216"
```

- **options**: This method returns all the current configuration options in a hash for the `session` object:

```
session.options # =>
{
  :path=>"/",
  :domain=>nil,
  :expire_after=>2592000,
  :secure=>false,
  :httponly=>true,
  :defer=>false,
  :renew=>false,
  :sidbits=>128,
  :secure_random=>SecureRandom,
  :secret=>"qwqweqwe24234k23j4lk2j42mnj2j4j4234j2l4n23",
  :old_secret=>"nnrmn23nl2j4l2k3j42k42314j231423n4n32l4j2",
  :coder=>#<Rack::Session::Cookie::Base64::Marshal:0x007fb13a
cf7018>
}
```

- **loaded?**: This is used to check whether the session is loaded for the application or not.

- **has_key? / key?**: Both of these methods can be used to check whether a particular key exists in the session; in other words, whether a key-value pair exists in the session for the provided key:

```
session.has_key? 'foo'      # => false
session.has_key? 'user_id'  # => true
```

- **keys**: This method returns all the keys that exist in the `session` object:

```
session.keys # => ["session_id", "user_id"]
```

  Right now, my `session` object has only two key-value pairs, `session_id`, which Sinatra creates automatically for every session object, and `user_id` that I saved to figure out the current user for the request.

- **entries**: This method returns all the entries that currently exist in the `session` object:

```
 session.entries # =>
[["session_id", "2ce00a5a97e51374083ab15a623f6826d755fa55b9912f2
ef703df72b5142216"], ["user_id", 5]]
```

- **clear**: This method is used to clear the session. It removes all the data stored in the `session` object.

- **delete**: This method is used to delete a particular key-value pair from the `session` object. This method accepts a key as an argument returns value is the returned value:

```
session.delete 'foo' # => "bar"
```

Handling authentication using session

You have learned about the `session` object and its methods; now we know that if we need to store something across the requests, we can store it in the session. In this section, you will learn how to build a simple authentication system for your application using sessions.

What is authentication and authorization?

Authentication is a process that ensures and confirms a user's identity based on the provided credentials (username and password). On the basis of the username and password, we can figure out that the user with the provided credentials exists, we have found our current user for the request, and this user will be called an authenticated user.

Authorization is the process of giving individuals access to objects in the system based on their identity. In other words, here we check whether the user with correct credentials has the correct rights or permissions for the requested action. For example, if we have several roles in our system, then we check whether the current user has the correct role to perform the action and is authorized to do the requested action.

This is the basic definition/description to understand the concept; now let's see this in terms of code for our application. Users have to authenticate in order to use our application using his/her credentials and must be authorized to perform actions such as deleting list items. (A user should not be able to delete the list items that don't belong to him/her).

Building authentication

Let's build a simple authentication system for our application. We know that we have a `User` model that stores the user's credentials, username, and password that was chosen at the time of signup.

As we know, HTTP is a stateless protocol and the server doesn't know about the previous requests and state of user as such, but we will store the user's information `user_id` in the session once a user has successfully signed in with the correct credentials. We will check this `user_id` in the `session` object on the server side before almost all requests; if it exists, it means that the user is already logged in, and if `user_id` doesn't exist in the session, then we will redirect the user to the login page.

To achieve this check of authentication, we can write a `before` block and apply our magic of authentication. Here is the code for this:

```
....
before do
    if !['login', 'signup'].include?(request.path_info.split('/')[1])
and session[:user_id].nil?
        redirect '/login'
    end
  end
```

This `before` block will be executed before every request. We have to skip our redirection code for the `login` and `signup` requests and this is what we are doing here. Skip the request and redirect it to the `login` page if we don't have `user_id` saved in the `session` object.

Now we need to give users a page for authentication where they will enter their credentials and log in to the system, and we have a `login.haml` page for this:

```
.col-md-4.col-md-offset-4
  .has-below
  .panel.panel-primary
    .panel-heading
      %h3.panel-title Login
    .panel-body
      %form.form-horizontal{name: "login", method: "post", action:
url("/login")}
```

```
.form-group
  %label.control-label.col-md-3{for: "name"} Username
  .col-md-8
    %input.form-control{type: "text", name: "name"}
.form-group
  %label.control-label.col-md-3{for: "password"} Password
  .col-md-8
    %input.form-control{type: "password", name: "password"}
.form-group
  .col-md-2.col-md-offset-3
    %button.btn.btn-sm.btn-primary{type: "submit"}
      %i.glyphicon.glyphicon-ok
      Submit
%a{href: '/signup'} Signup
```

We have already discussed this in detail, so we will focus on a few important lines very quickly:

Line 7: We are specifying the URL where this form is going to submit

Line 11: This creates an input field where users will write their username

Line 15: This creates an input field where users will write their password to log in

Now, the user can fill in the credentials and send the request back to the server where we have to handle it and save user_id in case of correct credentials; otherwise, we show an error message. The following is the code for this:

```
....
post '/login/?' do
  # validate user credentials
  md5sum = Digest::MD5.hexdigest params[:password]
  user = User.first(name: params[:name], password: md5sum)
  if user.nil?
    haml :error, locals: {error: 'Invalid login credentials'}
  else
    session[:user_id] = user.id
    redirect '/'
  end
end
```

Lets have look at some few important lines very quickly:

Line 4: The password can never be stored as plain text, so at the time of creation, we saved it as its corresponding md5 hash. Similarly, to find out the current user for the given password, we have to convert the password provided by the user into an md5 hash so that it is in a comparable form with data that exists in the database for a password.

Lets have look at some few important lines very quickly:

Line 5: Here, we are finding the current user for the provided username and password md5 token.

Line 7: If the user variable is nil, this means that we are not able to find the user with the given credentials so render an error template in this case and show the error message.

Line 9: If we found a user for the provided credentials, then we store the user's ID as user_id in the session object so that we can use it in the later requests, as explained earlier in this chapter.

Line 10: Now that we have found the authenticated user and stored the information user_id in the session, we will redirect the user to the landing page of the application, where we show all the list items for the user.

So this was a very simple quick implementation of authentication.

Building authorization

We have a logged in user; now, for every request, let's talk about authorization. As you learned, authorization is all about the checking of whether the user is allowed to do the action and has the authority or permission to do the action or not.

To make sure that the permissions are enforced, we have already created a Permission model where we store permissions corresponding to user and list. We have our data in place so we can implement authorization with the Permission model. Let's look at the code that we saw in previous chapters for the home page:

```
get '/' do
  all_lists = List.all
  haml :lists, locals: {lists: all_lists}
end
```

Lets have look at some few important lines very quickly:

Line 3: Here, we are fetching all the lists and showing them to the user. We fetched the collection of lists and stored it in a local variable.

Line 4: Here, we are setting up the fetched collection of lists in the local hash for the `haml` view so that we can use them in the view file.

Now let's look at the corresponding view file, `lists.haml`:

```
%h1 Lists

- lists.each do |list|
  .list_link
    %a{href: "lists/#{list.id}"}
      = list.name
```

In this file, we are simply looping the collection of lists and creating links to the list show page. In this page, we will have the links of the lists with their names.

The special thing to notice here is that we are showing all the lists here, irrespective of the permissions of the user. So what if we want to show the user the lists for which the user has associated permissions? This is how we can enforce the authorization. The following is the code for this:

```
....
get '/' do
  user = User.first(id: session[:user_id])
  all_lists = List.association_join(:permissions).where('permissions.
user_id = ?', user.id)
  haml :lists, locals: {lists: all_lists}
end
```

Lets have look at some few important lines very quickly:

Line 3: We are fetching the current user from the session.

Line 4: Here, instead of fetching all of the lists, we are fetching only those list records where the user has a permission associated to it. We used the `associated_join` method here, which you learned in the previous chapter.

Line 5: This is the same as the previous code; we are passing the list collection to the `haml` view.

Summary

In this chapter, you have learned the basics of a session in general and how you can configure it with Sinatra, both with simple and advanced options. We covered the various useful methods of the `session` object. We discussed the meaning of authentication and authorization individually and then we implemented a basic authentication and authorization module for our application.

In the next chapter, you will learn deployment; how we can push and publish our application so that anyone can access it.

10
Deploying the App

In the previous chapter, you learned about sessions; what session is, how it works, how we can enable session with Sinatra, its advanced options, and various session manipulation methods. We then discussed authentication and authorization and the difference between them. We then built an authentication system using session.

Now that our application is ready with all the basic features, authentication, and authorization, let's put it somewhere so that my family, friends, or anyone can use it; let's deploy it.

In this chapter, you will learn how to deploy the application on a public server through the following topic:

* Deploying the app on Heroku

Deployment

At this stage, our app is ready, we are using it happily (doing all the stuff we want), and everything is on my machine. Life is easy, but what happens when a friend or cousin, after watching this, wants to use it on their machine? In other words, your app is ready and you want it to be used by anyone in the world. So to achieve this, you have to place it somewhere so that anyone can use it; this somewhere could be a public server. You have to set up your app there so that it can run and anyone can use it; this setting up process is called deployment.

Deployment includes all the operations and necessary changes required to prepare the app for a running environment and ready to be used by end customers.

To ensure that our app will deploy and run successfully, we must first ensure that all the components on which our app is dependent (such as configuration variables) are already installed on the remote server.

Thanks to Heroku, all the basic necessary setup is already done for us; we just need to push our code to Heroku and do some minor configuration changes, such as add the database connection settings.

What is Heroku?

Heroku is a cloud application platform (or Platform as a Service, also known as PaaS) where we are going to deploy our app. It is a new and easy way of building and deploying web apps. Heroku lets app developers spend their time on their application code, not on managing servers, deployment, ongoing operations, or scaling.

Getting started with Heroku

Here is the step-by-step process of getting started with Heroku.

Creating an account

To start with Heroku, you must create an account on Heroku in order to deploy code on it. It will be a free account so don't worry about supplying credit card information. They have a very cool pricing model: they don't charge you for your account; instead, they charge you for the services you are using. The initial-level services are free. Let's say that your app is getting very heavy traffic and the requests are getting choked in the processing because of the amount of traffic. You can increase the number of Heroku dynos and power up your processing resources to handle the traffic. Another example is that Heroku provides you with the database for free but when your database grows, you will have to upgrade it and buy a plan for it. Similarly, for other services, Heroku charges for the services you are using.

Setting up the command-line interface

After creating a Heroku account, the next thing that we need to do is to set up the **Command Line Interface** (CLI) for Heroku so that we can access and communicate with Heroku from our terminal. In order to set this up, you need to download and install the Heroku Toolbelt. You can download it from `https://toolbelt.heroku.com/`. It is available for all environments, Mac, Ubuntu, and even for Windows.

Once you have downloaded and installed Heroku Toolbelt, you are ready to use Heroku from your terminal. Let's start with authenticating on Heroku from your terminal and you can do this in Linux/Unix environments with the following command:

```
$   heroku login
```

You will be prompted for your e-mail and the password to your Heroku account. On successful authentication, you will be shown the following success message:

```
$   Authentication successful.
```

Now your Heroku CLI is ready.

Creating a Heroku app

Now that our terminal is ready and we have logged in to Heroku via Heroku Toolbelt, let's create an app on Heroku for our todo app.

First, go to the app folder of your app using the `cd` (change directory) command:

```
$   cd path/to/todo
```

Next, create a Heroku app using the following command:

```
$   heroku create
```

It will create an app on Heroku and you will see something like this on your terminal:

```
Creating murmuring-brook-6173... done, stack is cedar-14

https://murmuring-brook-6173.herokuapp.com/ | https://git.heroku.com/
murmuring-brook-6173.git

Git remote heroku added
```

So the question should be, what is this? Actually, the `heroku` command created an app for you on Heroku for our todo app and did some other stuff for you, such as assigning a random name to the app and creating a subdomain with that name so that you (or anyone else) can access it from anywhere on the Internet with that subdomain.

Now, if you try to browse to the given URL on Heroku, you will see something like the following on your browser:

This means that our Heroku app is ready for the world; we just need to add our code here and we are ready to go.

Now, all you have to do is just commit (https://git-scm.com/docs/git-commit) the code and push it to Heroku. After committing the code, you can push it to Heroku with the following command; here, you are deploying your app's code to Heroku:

```
$  git push heroku master
```

You will see something like this on your terminal:

```
Counting objects: 80, done.

Delta compression using up to 4 threads.

Compressing objects: 100% (73/73), done.

Writing objects: 100% (80/80), 184.07 KiB | 0 bytes/s, done.

Total 80 (delta 30), reused 0 (delta 0)

remote: Compressing source files... done.

remote: Building source:

remote:

remote: -----> Ruby app detected

remote: -----> Compiling Ruby/Rack

remote: -----> Using Ruby version: ruby-2.0.0

remote: -----> Installing dependencies using bundler 1.9.7

remote:         Running: bundle install --without development:test --path
vendor/bundle --binstubs vendor/bundle/bin -j4 --deployment

remote:         Fetching gem metadata from https://rubygems.org/.........

remote:         Fetching version metadata from https://rubygems.org/..

remote:         Rubygems 2.0.14 is not threadsafe, so your gems must be
installed one at a time. Upgrade to Rubygems 2.1.0 or higher to enable
parallel gem installation.

remote:         Installing columnize 0.9.0

remote:         Installing byebug 5.0.0

remote:         Installing tilt 2.0.1

remote:         Installing haml 4.0.6

remote:         Installing mysql 2.9.1

remote:         Installing rack 1.6.4

remote:         Installing rack-protection 1.5.3

remote:         Installing sequel 4.25.0

remote:         Installing sinatra 1.4.6

remote:         Using bundler 1.9.7
```

```
remote:          Bundle complete! 6 Gemfile dependencies, 10 gems now
installed.

remote:          Gems in the groups development and test were not
installed.

remote:          Bundled gems are installed into ./vendor/bundle.

remote:          Post-install message from haml:

remote:          HEADS UP! Haml 4.0 has many improvements, but also has
changes that may break

remote:          your application:

remote:          * Support for Ruby 1.8.6 dropped

remote:          * Support for Rails 2 dropped

remote:          * Sass filter now always outputs <style> tags

remote:          * Data attributes are now hyphenated, not underscored

remote:          * html2haml utility moved to the html2haml gem

remote:          * Textile and Maruku filters moved to the haml-contrib gem

remote:          For more info see:

remote:          http://rubydoc.info/github/haml/haml/file/CHANGELOG.md

remote:          Bundle completed (16.55s)

remote:          Cleaning up the bundler cache.

remote: -----> Writing config/database.yml to read from DATABASE_URL

remote:

remote: ###### WARNING:

remote:          You have not declared a Ruby version in your Gemfile.

remote:          To set your Ruby version add this line to your Gemfile:

remote:          ruby '2.0.0'

remote:          # See https://devcenter.heroku.com/articles/ruby-versions
for more information.

remote:

remote: ###### WARNING:

remote:          No Procfile detected, using the default web server
(webrick)

remote:          https://devcenter.heroku.com/articles/ruby-default-web-
server

remote:

remote: -----> Discovering process types

remote:          Procfile declares types -> (none)

remote:          Default types for Ruby  -> console, rake, web

remote:
```

```
remote: -----> Compressing... done, 17.9MB
remote: -----> Launching... done, v4
remote:            https://murmuring-brook-6173.herokuapp.com/ deployed to
Heroku
remote:
remote: Verifying deploy.... done.
To https://git.heroku.com/murmuring-brook-6173.git
* [new branch]       master -> master
```

Here, our code is getting pushed to Heroku; then, Heroku found that our app requires a Ruby server. It is preparing the Ruby environment and then installing the gems that we are using in our app. (We specified our gems in the Gemfile.) It then shows some warnings related to gems and finally launches our app with the domain name of the app (https://murmuring-brook-6173.herokuapp.com/).

Now, you can go and check the application by browsing the URL. Alternatively, you can open it through your terminal with the following command:

```
$  heroku open
```

This will open your app in the browser for you.

Wait, you are getting an application error page, right? Don't worry, this is expected! Now you might think that everything was working on my machine but what happened when I deployed to heroku? The answer is that we need to prepare our app to be able to run on Heroku. These are one-time setup items that we are now going to discuss.

Setting up an app for Heroku

Here are the steps to set up your app on Heroku.

Adding Ruby to Gemfile

Add the ruby version to your Gemfile as follows:

```
source 'https://rubygems.org'


ruby "2.0.0"


gem 'bundler', '1.10.6'
gem 'sinatra', '1.4.6'
gem 'sequel', '4.25.0'
```

This will tell Heroku the proper Ruby version for our app.

Adding Procfile

On our local machine, we are running our app using the `rackup` command, but how would Heroku know about the app startup command? In `Procfile`, we specify it and tell Heroku to execute it. In **Procfile**, we are declaring what commands are run by your application's dynos on the Heroku platform. If you bought multiple dynos from Heroku, then you can declare multiple processes here in this file. Our `Procfile` will look as follows:

```
web: bundle exec rackup config.ru -p $PORT
```

This is a single process command for web. The **web** keyword tells Heroku that this process type will be used for the HTTP routing stack of Heroku and receive web requests when the app is deployed.

Using SQL on Heroku

We already set up SQL for our local machine and we have to perform a similar activity for the Heroku app. However, we cannot install or uninstall this directly on Heroku, so instead, we will add add-ons for this. Everything on Heroku is available as an add-on as this is their model for their platform services (such as databases). Whenever you need an additional service, you need to enable its add-on. So, let's add the add-on for SQL, but for a free account, Heroku only provides the PostgreSQL database! Not a problem; let's use it for production. This is the power of using **Object-relational mapping (ORM)**, we just change the adapter and its settings and we are ready to use the new database. To enable the SQL add-on, we need to run the following command:

```
$   heroku addons:create heroku-postgresql
```

This will add the free PostgreSQL database to our app. Now we need to change our app's database configuration options for this production environment.

For PostgreSQL configuration options, you need to log in to the Heroku account in the browser, select the current app, and navigate to the PostgreSQL add-on, where you will find your database's connection settings. However, we should never add production database settings to the code base because it contains all the database credentials! Anyone viewing our source code repository (if we are using GitHub) could easily view our database credentials, so we use will Heroku's configuration variables here.

We can add configuration variables to our Heroku app from the command line and then use them in the code. Let's see how we can do this:

```
$ heroku config:set HOST='ec2-184-****-****.compute-1.amazonaws.com'
$ heroku config:set DATABASE=db******
$ heroku config:set USER=********
$ heroku config:set PORT=5432
$ heroku config:set PASSWORD=pjs8qm-*******
```

Here, we set all the database-related options in the app's config vars of Heroku; you can also check and modify them from the Heroku web interface.

Now let's add the new production configuration block to our database.yml file:

```
development:
    adapter: 'mysql'
    host: 'localhost'
    database: 'todo_development'
    user: 'root'
    password: 'password'


production:
    adapter: 'postgres'
    host: ENV['HOST']
    database: ENV['DATABASE']
    user: ENV['USER']
    password: ENV['PASSWORD']
    port: ENV['PORT']
```

Here, we are using all of the previously added Heroku configuration variables.

If you try to deploy at this stage, your application will fail because the YML files that Heroku generates are actually ERB files and we need to parse them first before using them. We are currently using the YAML file in our app.rb file for the database initialization, so we have to modify it as follows:

```
require 'sinatra'
require 'sequel'
class Todo < Sinatra::Base
  ....
  configure do
    env = ENV['RACK_ENV']
```

```
    DB = Sequel.connect YAML.load(ERB.new( File.read(File.
join("config","database.yml"))).result)[env]

    Dir[File.join(File.dirname(__FILE__),'models','*.rb')].each {
|model| require model }
  end
  ....
end
```

We changed line 7 of the code, where we parsed it first from ERB and then YAML.

We also have to update our Gemfile to add a new gem 'pg' for the PostgreSQL adapter in the production environment:

```
source 'https://rubygems.org'
ruby "2.0.0"

gem 'bundler', '1.10.6'
gem 'sinatra', '1.4.6'
gem 'sequel', '4.25.0'
gem 'mysql', '2.9.1' #For MySQL
gem 'haml', '4.0.6'

group :production do
  gem 'pg'
end
```

Now our app is ready. We can commit the code and deploy it again with the deployment commands:

```
$  git add .
$  git commit -m 'update production database settings for Heroku'
$  git push heroku master
```

This will deploy the app and you will be able to see the login page. Unfortunately, when you try to sign up, the app will crash again! Any idea why? You can check the Heroku logs with the following command:

```
$  heroku logs
```

When you look at the logs closely, it will show you that the table doesn't exist yet. The reason for this is that we have attached the new database to the production app but we haven't run the migrations for the production database yet. We have to run the migrations so that our production database will have the required tables in place.

To run the migrations on Heroku, we need to access the Heroku `bash` and run the migrations there. Here is the command for it:

```
$   heroku run bash
```

With this command, you will be logged in to Heroku's `bash` and you need run the migration command just like you ran it locally earlier. Here is the command:

```
$   sequel -m db/migrations/ postgres://ns***:pjs8qm22-***@ec…
```

The last argument is your database URL, which you can find out from Heroku's configuration variables (either from the web view or CLI). The command in the command line interface is as follows:

```
$   heroku config
```

This will show you the all configuration variables for your Heroku app; its output will be something like the following:

```
=== murmuring-brook-6173 Config Vars
DATABASE:       db****
DATABASE_URL: postgres://ns***:***....
HOST:           ec2-****
LANG:           en_US.UTF-8
PASSWORD:       ****
PORT:           5432
RACK_ENV:       production
USER:           ******
```

Now our app is deployed and ready. Anyone can use it. On the Internet, they can sign up and start creating lists.

Summary

In this chapter, you have learned about deployment, what Heroku is, and how we can use Heroku to deploy our app. You have also learned the initial setup steps that we need to do on Heroku, various Heroku commands, and their billing model.

Index

A

B

C

D

data
sending 68
database connection
associations 113
callbacks 112
establishing 99-101
hooks 112
interactive console 102
ORM, using 103
Sequel model 103
data types, Ruby
array 12
hash 14
numbers 11, 12
strings 11
symbols 12
db_schema method 104
def_column_alias method 106
delete method 111
deployment 127
destroy method 111

E

eager loading
of associations 113
Entity-Relationship Diagram (ERD) 113
eql? function 25
equal? function 25
errors method 109
exception handling 27, 28
exists? method 110

F

file structure, ToDo app
app.rb 31
bundle install 32
bundler 31
config.ru 31
Gemfile 31
gem install bundler 32
lib/routes.rb 32
route 32
finder method 107
find_or_create method 105

first method 106
first! method 106
Fixnum.times 26
for..in 26
forms
creating 87
data, handling in backend 93, 94
HTML form tag 87, 88
new_list.haml, writing 88-92
validations 94
frontend validations 94, 95

G

Gemfile
about 31
Ruby, adding to 133
gem install bundler 32
git-commit
URL 130

H

hash
about 14
hash.each 15
hash.include? 15
hash.keys 15
hash.select 15
Hello World application 29
Heroku
account, creating 128
Command Line Interface (CLI),
setting up 128, 129
Heroku app, creating 129-132
SQL, using 133-136
ToDo app, setting up 132
Heroku Toolbelt
URL 128
hooks
defining 112
HTML Abstraction Markup Language (HAML)
about 5, 68, 80
installing 5
haml templates, writing 80, 81
using, in Sinatra application 5, 6
versus HTML 5

to_hash method 109
Twitter Bootstrap
  about 79, 80
  URL 42

U

unless..end 23
unrestrict_primary_key method 108
until-end 25
update_all method 112
update method 112
User model
  defining 48
  responsibilities 55, 56
users module 38
users table
  created_at 39
  id 39
  name 39
  password 39
  username 39

V

validations
  backend validations 95, 96
  frontend validations 95

valid? method 109
values method 109
views
  designing 41, 68
  list, editing 70, 71
  list permissions, modifying 73, 74
  list, updating 71, 72
  login page, displaying 75
  new list, saving 69, 70
  page, displaying for all existing lists 68
  page, displaying for new list creation 69
  signup page, displaying 74
  user data, saving 74
  user login, handling 75
  user logout, handling 76

W

while-end 25
Windows
  Ruby, installing 10

Y

YAML
  about 100
  URL 100

Printed in Great Britain
by Amazon

56158506R00095